Congressional
Research
Service

The Role of Local Food Systems in U.S. Farm Policy

Renée Johnson
Specialist in Agricultural Policy

Randy Alison Aussenberg
Analyst in Nutrition Assistance Policy

Tadlock Cowan
Analyst in Natural Resources and Rural Development

July 17, 2014

Congressional Research Service

7-5700

www.crs.gov

R42155

CRS Report for Congress
Prepared for Members and Committees of Congress

Summary

Sales of locally produced foods comprise a small but growing part of U.S. agricultural sales. USDA estimates that farm-level value of local food sales totaled about $4.8 billion in 2008, or about 1.6% of the U.S. market for agricultural products. An estimated total of 107,000 farms are engaged in local food systems, or about 5% of all U.S. farms.

There is no established definition of what constitutes a "local food." Local and regional food systems generally refer to agricultural production and marketing that occurs within a certain geographic proximity (between farmer and consumer) or that involves certain social or supply chain characteristics in producing food (such as small family farms, urban gardens, or farms using sustainable agriculture practices). Some perceive locally sourced foods as fresher and higher in quality compared to some other readily available foods, and also believe that purchasing local foods helps support local farm economies and/or farmers that use certain production practices that are perceived to be more environmentally sustainable.

A wide range of farm businesses may be considered to be engaged in local foods. These include direct-to-consumer marketing, farmers' markets, farm-to-school programs, community-supported agriculture, community gardens, school gardens, food hubs and market aggregators, and kitchen incubators and mobile slaughter units. Other types of operations include on-farm sales/stores, internet marketing, food cooperatives and buying clubs, pick-your-own or "U-Pick" operations, roadside farm stands, urban farms (and rooftop farms and gardens), community kitchens, small-scale food processing and decentralized root cellars, and some agritourism or other types of on-farm recreational activities.

Many existing federal programs benefiting U.S. agricultural producers may also provide support and assistance for local food systems. These include farm support and grant programs administered by the U.S. Department of Agriculture (USDA), and may be grouped into several broad program categories: marketing and promotion; business assistance; rural and community development; nutrition and education; agricultural research and cooperative extension; and farmland conservation. Examples include USDA's farmers' market programs, rural cooperative grants, and selected child nutrition programs, among myriad other grant and loan programs, as well as USDA's research and cooperative extension service. In addition, the 2008 farm bill (P.L. 110-246, Food, Conservation, and Energy Act of 2008) contained a few program provisions that directly support local and regional food systems. The 2014 farm bill (P.L. 113-79, Agricultural Act of 2014) reauthorized and expanded many of these provisions. Although the 2008 and 2014 farm bills contained some specific programs that directly support local and regional food systems, many community and farm advocacy groups have argued that such food systems should play a larger policy role within the next farm bill, and that laws should be modified to reflect broader, more equitable policies across a range of production systems, including local food systems. The local impact of new and existing programs may depend on appropriated funding and the nature of implementation.

Contents

Figures

Tables

Appendixes

Contacts

Introduction

Sales of locally produced foods comprise a small, but growing, part of U.S. agricultural sales. The U.S. Department of Agriculture (USDA) estimates that farm-level value of local food sales totaled about $4.8 billion in 2008, about 1.6% of the U.S. market for agricultural products. An estimated total of 107,000 farms were engaged in local food systems, about 5% of all U.S. farms. Examples of the types of farming businesses that are engaged in local foods are direct-to-consumer marketing, farmers' markets, farm-to-school programs, community-supported agriculture, community gardens, school gardens, food hubs and market aggregators, and kitchen incubators and mobile slaughter units, among myriad other types of operations.

Many existing federal programs benefiting U.S. agricultural producers provide support and assistance for local and regional food systems.[1] These include USDA farm support and grant programs that may be grouped into the following broad program categories: marketing and promotion; business assistance; rural and community development; nutrition and education; agricultural research and cooperative extension; and farmland conservation. In addition, both the 2014 farm bill (P.L. 113-79, Agricultural Act of 2014) and the 2008 farm bill (P.L. 110-246, Food, Conservation, and Energy Act of 2008) contained provisions that directly support local and regional food systems. Other introduced legislation in the 112th and 113th Congress would further expand upon these types of existing programs to create additional opportunities for local and regional food systems.

Many community and farm advocacy groups have argued that such food systems should play a larger policy role within the farm bill, and that the laws should be reformed to reflect broader, more equitable policies across a range of production systems, including local and regional food systems. Supporters of local foods cite the increasing popularity of local foods, given perceived higher product quality and freshness, and a general belief that purchasing local foods helps support local farm economies and/or farmers that use certain production practices that may be more environmentally sustainable. They also contend that subsidizing the more traditional agriculture producers creates a competitive disadvantage to other producers who do not receive such support. Those opposed to extending farm bill benefits to local food systems cite concerns about limited financial resources to support U.S. agriculture and the perceived need to support the most efficient and productive farms. Other criticisms highlight the perception that USDA's support of local foods is mostly targeted to affluent consumers in urban areas, rather than farmers.

This report is organized into three parts. First, it provides background on local and regional food systems, focusing on available data on direct-to-consumer sales, farmers' markets, farm-to-school programs, community-supported agriculture (CSA),[2] and community gardens. Second, it highlights available resources within existing federal programs administered by USDA and other

---

[1] For the purposes of this report, "local and regional food systems" refers to systems in which foods are marketed directly to the consumer, or in which the identity of the farm where the food is produced is preserved in some way (often referred to "farm identity-preserved marketing"). USDA definitions of "direct-to-consumer" sales and "direct" sales to consumers are not strictly equivalent: direct-to-consumer sales are defined as the value of agricultural products sold directly to individuals for human consumption (e.g., from roadside stands, farmers' markets, and U-pick sites), but exclude agricultural products sold through their own processing and marketing operations (e.g., catalog or internet sales) and nonedible products, which may be included as part of "direct" sales.

[2] As is discussed later in this report, a CSA provides a way for consumers to buy local, seasonal food directly from a farm by pledging to support that farm's costs and risks at the beginning of each year in return for a share of that farm's annual production.

---

agencies that may be applied to support local food systems. It also describes some of the Obama Administration's initiatives that leverage existing USDA programs to support local food systems. (A more comprehensive table and description of existing programs is included in the **Appendix**.) Finally, this report discusses some of the legislative options that have been proposed by Congress and intended to broaden support for local and regional food systems. Some aspects of these proposals have been included as part of the reauthorization of the periodic farm bill.

Local Food Markets

Estimated Market Size

In recent years, growing demand for "local" foods has raised the importance of direct farm sales and the marketing of locally grown foods within the U.S. agricultural sector. Although local food sales still comprise a small share of overall sales, demand continues to grow. USDA estimated that the farm-level value of local food sales totaled about $4.8 billion in 2008, from both direct-to-consumer sales and intermediated sales (**Figure 1**). Of this total, direct-to-consumer sales accounted for $0.9 billion, and intermediated sales (through local grocers, restaurants, and regional distributors) accounted for $2.7 billion in local food sales.[3] Farms using both direct and intermediated marketing channels accounted for another $1.2 billion in sales. Compared to a total farm-level value of all U.S. agricultural production estimated at about $300 billion, the local foods segment of the market accounted for about 1.6% of the U.S. market for agricultural products.[4] An estimated total of 107,000 farms were engaged in local food systems, about 5% of all U.S. farms.[5]

The popularity of and demand for local foods continues to grow. Survey results reported by the National Restaurant Association indicate that locally sourced meats and seafood and locally grown produce are among the top menu trends for 2012, followed by healthful kids' meals and locally sourced foods and ingredients.[6] Locally grown and organic foods are also expected to be among the trends with the greatest growth potential in the produce industry.[7] Some major food retailers, such as Walmart, also have stated their intentions to increases their purchases of locally sourced produce and food from small and medium farmers, along with other steps intended to increase the availability of fresh fruits and vegetables to consumers.[8]

---

[3] S. Low and S. Vogel, *Direct and Intermediated Marketing of Local Foods in the United States*, ERR-128, USDA Economic Research Service (ERS), November 2011; and "Local Foods Marketing Channels Encompass a Wide Range of Producers," *Amber Waves*, December 2011.

[4] USDA, *Census of Agriculture*, 2007, Table 2. Data are for 2007.

[5] Ibid. There were an estimated total of 2.2 million U.S. farms in 2007.

[6] "Children's Nutrition, Local Foods to Top Menu Trends," *Food Business News*, December 8, 2011. Based on a survey of 1,800 professional chefs who are members of the American Culinary Federation. Also, "Locally Sourced Meats among Top Menu Trends for 2011," *Meatingplace*, November 2, 2010.

[7] Informal feedback to Fresh Produce Industry discussion group, November 14, 2011.

[8] "Walmart Unveils Global Sustainable Agriculture Goals," October 14, 2010, press release; "Walmart ramping up fresh food marketing push next year" *Agri-Pulse*, December 2011.

Figure 1. USDA Estimates of Local Food Sales

(farm value, 2008)

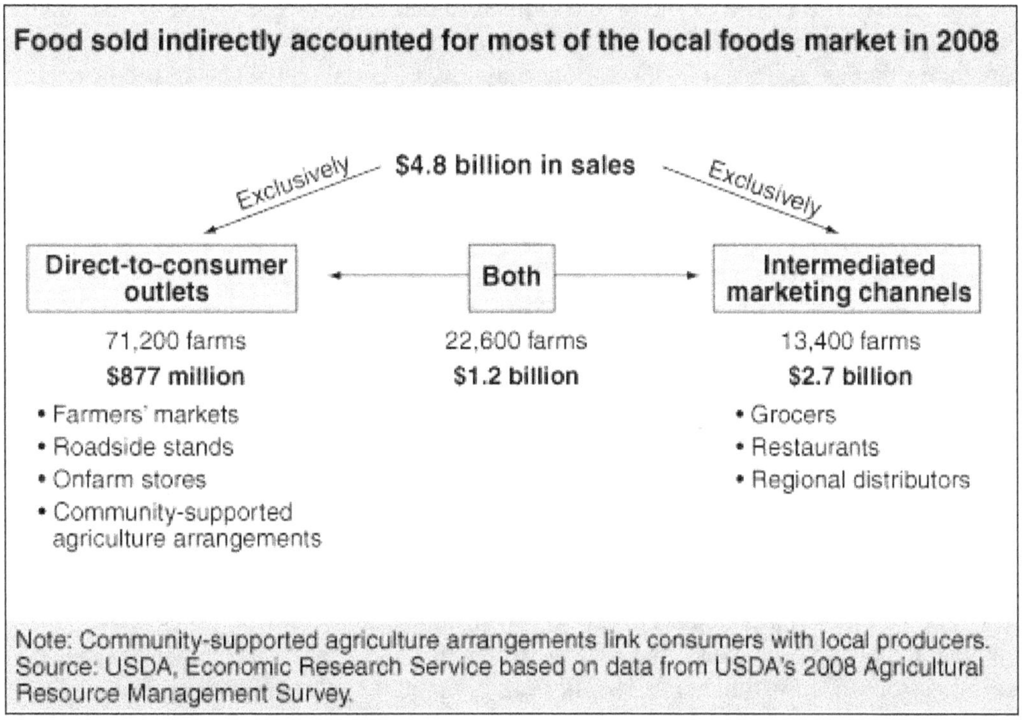

Food sold indirectly accounted for most of the local foods market in 2008

Exclusively — **$4.8 billion in sales** — Exclusively

Direct-to-consumer outlets	Both	Intermediated marketing channels
71,200 farms	22,600 farms	13,400 farms
$877 million	**$1.2 billion**	**$2.7 billion**
• Farmers' markets		• Grocers
• Roadside stands		• Restaurants
• Onfarm stores		• Regional distributors
• Community-supported agriculture arrangements		

Note: Community-supported agriculture arrangements link consumers with local producers.
Source: USDA, Economic Research Service based on data from USDA's 2008 Agricultural Resource Management Survey.

Source: S. Low and S. Vogel, "Local Foods Marketing Channels Encompass a Wide Range of Producers," *Amber Waves*, December 2011.

Definitions of Local Foods

The focus on locally sourced foods and efforts to convince consumers to "buy local" are not new concepts. "State grown" or "locally grown" programs were introduced in the 1930s, and such programs now exist in most U.S. states.[9] In the late 1990s, the USDA-appointed National Commission on Small Farms, among other recommendations, emphasized the need to strengthen the "local farm economy" through policy changes within the department's federal programs as a way to better meet the needs of small farmers and ranchers.[10] Although consumer interest in local foods has some of its roots in the late 1960s and concerns about the environment, growth in mainstream consumer demand has increased sharply in the past decade, along with consumer willingness to pay more for such products.

Despite the growing popularity of the local foods market, there is no established definition of what constitutes a "local food."[11] There is also no consensus about what primary factors would need to be considered if one were to construct a definition of what constitutes a "local food."

---

[9] Wuyang Hu, et al., "What Is Local and For What Foods Does It Matter," paper presented at the Southern Agricultural Economics Association annual Meeting in Orlando Florida, February 6-9, 2010.

[10] USDA, "A Time to Act," National Commission on Small Farms report and recommendations, July 2009.

[11] See S. Martinez et al., *Local Food Systems: Concepts, Impacts, and Issues*, ERR-97, USDA, ERS, May 2010, and R. King, "Theme Overview: Local Food—Perceptions, Prospects, and Policies," *Choices* magazine, Quarter 1, 2010.

In most cases, local foods refer to foods produced near where they are consumed, based on a certain geographic proximity (between farmer and consumer) or the number of miles the food travels from where it is grown to where it is ultimately purchased or consumed by the end user. Local foods may also refer to the types of marketing channels used between farmers and consumer. In other cases, however, local foods may invoke certain attributes desired by the consumers who purchase them, involving certain social or supply-chain characteristics in producing food, such as supporting small family farms, urban gardens, or farms using sustainable agriculture practices.[12] The latter case also raises questions about how the local food movement may be used to address a perceived need, such as increasing access to fresh, nutritious foods for underserved communities, or contributing to rural economic development. The lack of a universally agreed-upon definition, however, does raise questions about "what is a local food" and may also provide opportunities for fraud in the marketplace with the sale of foods that are marketed as "local" when they cannot be determined to be local.[13]

"Local" Based on Distance Traveled

Though "local" has a geographic connotation, there is no consensus on the distance or number of miles between production and consumption. USDA reports that, depending on the definition, distances can vary widely, from 25 miles up to 350 miles from where the "local" food is produced.[14] The single statutory definition for "locally or regionally produced agricultural food product" in the United States applies to products transported less than 400 miles or within the state in which they are produced.[15] In Canada, fresh fruits and vegetables cannot be labeled as "local" unless produced within about 31 miles (50 kilometers) of where they are sold.[16] Most state definitions view "local" to mean grown within state borders; however, in some cases "local" may be defined as food grown within a certain geographic region that might cross state lines. Definitions based on geographic distance vary depending on the state or region and on whether the food is fresh or processed, among other factors.[17]

Most consumers, when they purchase local foods, have been shown to generally believe that their local purchases are sourced within a much smaller distance from where it is produced—generally under 100 miles—even though this may not actually be the case.[18] Generally, consumers believe that locally marketed foods are produced on nearby small farms.

Two recently enacted U.S. federal laws provide different definitions of "local" based on the geographic distance between food production and sales. These definitions differ in terms of the number of miles the food may be transported, but both require that food be sold within the state where it is produced to be considered local. The 2008 farm bill (as noted above) defined the term

---

[12] As discussed later in this report, USDA has identified three pillars of sustainability: profit over the long term; stewardship of our nation's land, air and water; and quality of life for farmers, ranchers, and their communities. USDA SARE, "What Is Sustainable Agriculture?" http://www.sare.org/.

[13] See, for example: "States on Lookout for Local Produce That Isn't," *The Packer*, June 29, 2010.

[14] M. Hand, "Local Food Systems: Emerging Research and Policy Issues," USDA conference, June 26, 2009.

[15] Food, Conservation, and Energy Act of 2008, P.L. 110-246, §6015. This definition applies to eligibility under a USDA's Business and Industry loan program, but has also been applied by USDA to other programs in cases where a specific statutory definition has not been defined.

[16] Canadian Food Inspection Agency, " 'Local' Claim on Fresh Fruits and Vegetables," http://www.inspection.gc.ca.

[17] C. Durham, et al., "Consumer Definitions of 'Locally Grown' for Fresh Fruits and Vegetables," *Journal of Food Distribution Research*, vol. 40, no. 1, March 2009.

[18] Wuyang Hu, et al., "What Is Local and For What Foods Does It Matter."

"locally or regionally produced agricultural food product," as it pertains to eligibility under a USDA loan program, to mean "any agricultural food product that is raised, produced, and distributed in ... the locality or region in which the final product is marketed, so that the total distance that the product is transported *is less than 400 miles from the origin of the product*"; or "any agricultural food product that is raised, produced, and distributed in ... *the State in which the product is produced.*"[19] Alternatively, food safety legislation enacted in 2010 defined a "qualified enduser"—for the purposes of exempting smaller, local producers from regulation—as "the consumer of the food; or ... a restaurant or retail food establishment ... that is *located ... in the same State as the farm that produced the food; or ... not more than 275 miles from such farm.*"[20]

A 2013 survey of buyers of local foods indicates that most consumers (64%) consider food "local" if produced within a 100-mile radius of the store, while other consumers (37%) consider products from the same state to be local.[21]

Elsewhere within USDA and other federal agencies, there are many examples of very specific statutory definitions for "farms" and "food facilities" that govern a range of programs and policies.[22] These definitions generally do not differentiate between the types of farms and food facilities based on the operation's various production practices, size, locality, or distance between production area and markets, among other types of producer- or consumer-driven attributes.

"Local" Based on Marketing Outlet

Another measure of "local food" is based on the types of marketing channels used by farmers to distribute food from the farm to the consumer.[23] USDA data are based on surveyed farm information of sales by selected marketing channels, including direct-to-consumer outlets and intermediated outlets. Direct-to-consumer marketing outlets include roadside stands, on-farm stores, farmers' markets, and CSAs. Intermediated outlets include grocers, restaurants, and regional distributors.[24] By value, the leading products that are directly marketed to consumers are nursery and greenhouse products, fruits and vegetables, and livestock and dairy products.[25]

Across all farms, local foods marketed through all channels totaled about $4.8 billion in 2008. Of this total, 18% (about $0.9 billion) was marketed through direct-to-consumer marketing outlets only, 57% (about $2.7 billion) was marketed through intermediated marketing outlets only, and another 25% (about $1.2 billion) was marketed through both types (**Figure 1**; **Table 1**). Farms with local food sales reported using 160,800 marketing channels to sell local food. The majority (75%) of these outlets were comprised of direct-to-consumer marketing outlets (such as farmers' markets, roadside stands, on-farm stores, and CSAs). Intermediated outlets (such as grocers, restaurants, and regional distributors) accounted for about 25% of all marketing channels used to sell local food (**Table 1**). Some differences reflect operation size based on the farm's annual sales.

---

[19] Food, Conservation, and Energy Act of 2008, P.L. 110-246, §6015. Italics added for emphasis.

[20] FDA Food Safety Modernization Act, P.L. 111-353, §105. Italics added for emphasis.

[21] A. T. Kearney, "Buying into the Local Food Movement," 2013. Online survey of 1,300 U.S. respondents.

[22] See, for example, CRS Report RL34612, *Food Safety on the Farm*.

[23] M. Hand and S. Martinez, "Just What Does Local Mean?" *Choices* magazine, Quarter 1, 2010; and S. Low and S. Vogel, *Direct and Intermediated Marketing of Local Foods in the United States*.

[24] Despite common perception, farmers' markets do not dominate direct farms sales (L. Lev and L. Gwin, "Filling in the Gaps: Eight Things to Recognize about Farm-Direct Marketing," *Choices* magazine, Quarter 1, 2010).

[25] USDA, "Direct Marketing Survey 2009," October 2010.

Most farms (81%) engaged in direct-to-consumer sales are "small" farms, with annual farm sales under $50,000, totaling an estimated 86,700 farms in 2008. Other USDA data indicate that among smaller farms (annual farm sales under $50,000) selling direct-to-consumer, the majority (80%) of these farms have gross sales under $5,000 per year.[26]

Table 1. Marketing Channels Used by Local Food Sales Farms, by Farm Size

Sales Channels	Small (sales less than $50,000)	Medium (sales of $50,000-$249,999)	Large (sales of $250,000 or more)	Total
Number of Farms with Local Food Sales	**86,728**	**15,202**	**5,301**	**107,229**
Share of Farms, by size category	5.3%	5.1%	2.5%	5.0%
Share of All Farms, with local sales	80.9%	14.2%	4.9%	100%
Local Food Sales:				
Marketed Through All Channels	11.1%	19.1%	69.8%	$4.8 billion
Direct-to-Consumer Outlets Only	33.7%	38.9%	27.4%	$0.9 billion
Intermediated Marketing Channels Only	3.5%	3.6%	92.9%	$2.7 billion
Both Marketing Channels	11.7%	39.5%	48.8%	$1.2 billion
Number of Local Food Sales Outlets Used	**121,198**	**15,202**	**5,301**	**160,795**
By Marketing Outlet (percent):	**100%**	**100%**	**100%**	**100%**
Direct-to-Consumer Outlets	**78.0%**	**70.7%**	**55.5%**	**75.3%**
Roadside Stands	34.1%	24.9%	23.7%	31.8%
Farmers' Markets	34.6%	25.9%	14.7%	31.8%
On-Farm Stores	8.3%	17.4%	15.7%	10.4%
CSAs	1.1%	2.5%	1.4%	1.3%
Intermediated Outlets	**22.0%**	**29.3%**	**45.0%**	**24.7%**
Grocers and Restaurants	17.2%	26.0%	23.7%	19.2%
Regional Distributors	4.8%	3.4%	21.4%	5.5%

Source: S. Low and S. Vogel, *Direct and Intermediated Marketing of Local Foods in the United States.* 2008 data. Data are as reported by USDA, although subtotals may not add up in all cases.

Notes: USDA definitions of "direct-to-consumer" marketing and "direct sales" to consumers are not strictly equivalent: direct-to-consumer sales are defined as the value of agricultural products sold directly to individuals for human consumption (for example, from roadside stands, farmers' markets, and U-pick sites), but exclude agricultural products sold through their own processing and marketing operations (such as catalog or internet sales) and nonedible products (which may be included as part of "direct" sales).

---

[26] USDA, AMS, *Facts on Direct-to-Consumer Food Marketing*, May 2009.

The leading states with direct-to-consumer marketing sales in 2007 were California, New York, Pennsylvania, Michigan, Oregon, Ohio, Washington, Wisconsin, Massachusetts, and Texas.[27] States where direct-to-consumer marketing comprised a large share of the state's total agricultural sales were Rhode Island, Massachusetts, New Hampshire, Connecticut, Vermont, New Jersey, Maine, Alaska, New York, and Hawaii. USDA reports that the value of direct-to-consumer food marketing increased in all U.S. producing regions from 1997 to 2007 (**Figure 2**).[28] **Figure 3** provides a county-level map showing the percentage of U.S. farms with direct sales in 2007.

Figure 2. Value of Direct-to-Consumer Food Marketing, by Region (1997-2007)

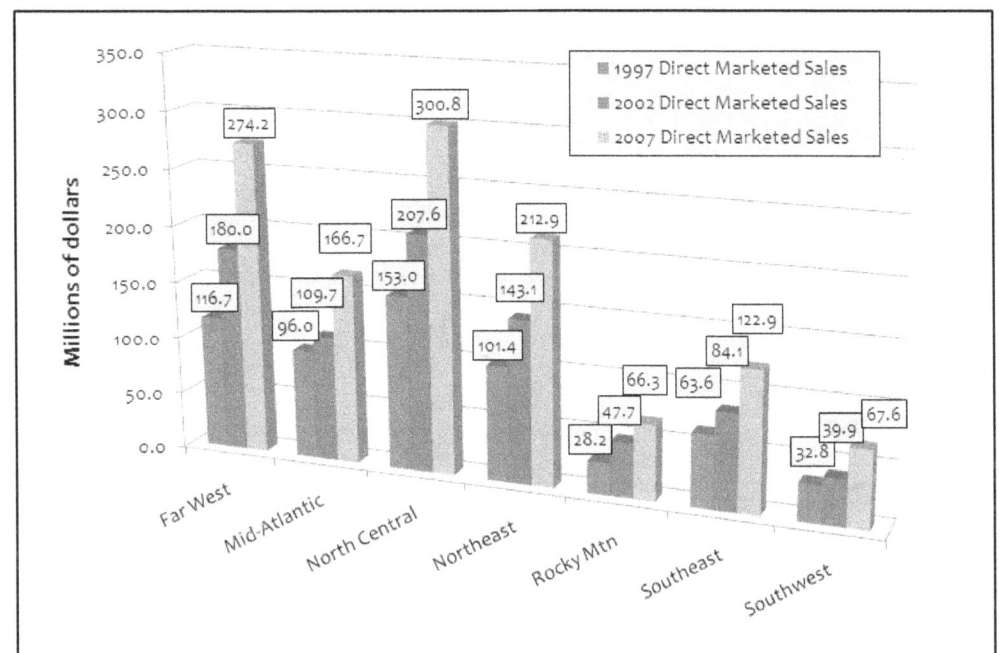

Source: USDA, Agricultural Marketing Service (AMS), *Facts on Direct-to-Consumer Food Marketing*, May 2009.

"Local" Based on Perceived Attributes

Myriad other factors influence consumer interest in local food systems. These are mostly based on consumer perceptions of certain desired social or supply-chain characteristics in producing "local" foods, such as production by a small family farm, an urban farm or garden, or a farm using sustainable agriculture practices. Many of these factors dovetail into some of the other reasons influencing growing demand for local foods. (As discussed in the text box below, marketing of local foods differs from so-called geographical indications, which are also used to market agricultural products.)

---

[27] Ibid.

[28] Ibid. Other resources are at Agricultural Marketing Resource Center (AgMRC), "Direct Marketing" (www.agmrc.org)

Geographical Indications

Demand for local foods is generally driven by a product's perceived quality and reputation, among other desired attributes, often associated with where or how the product is produced. In this way local foods may be viewed as similar to foods carrying geographical indications (GIs); however, GIs are often more strictly defined and also may be registered under administrative trademark structures governed by the U.S. Patent and Trademark Office (PTO).

"Geographical indications" (GI) are place names (or, in some countries, words associated with a place) used to identify the origin and quality, reputation, or other characteristics of products. Like trademarks, GIs are source-identifiers; guarantees of quality; and valuable business interests. Specific examples of geographical indications from the United States include Florida oranges; Idaho potatoes; Napa Valley wines; Missouri Pecans; and Washington State apples. Other GI examples in European markets include Champagne; Parma ham; and Roquefort cheese.

Within the context of the World Trade Organization (WTO), GIs are defined in Article 22(1) of the WTO's Trade Related Aspects of Intellectual Property Rights (TRIPS) agreement as "indications which identify a good as originating in the territory of a Member, or a region or locality in that territory, where a given quality, reputation or other characteristic of the good is essentially attributable to its geographic origin." GIs were first negotiated in the WTO as part of the 1994 Uruguay Round, which introduced intellectual property rules into the multilateral trading system.

GIs protect consumers from deceptive or misleading labels, and provide consumers with choices among products and with information on which to base their choices. Producers benefit because GIs give them recognition for the distinctiveness of their products in the market. Agricultural producers are increasingly recognizing that GIs serve as commercially valuable marketing tools within the global economy, similar to other forms of intellectual property. As intellectual property, GIs are eligible for relief from acts of infringement and/or unfair competition. The use of geographical indications for wines and cheese products particularly—which some countries consider to be protected intellectual property, and others consider to be generic or semi-generic terms—has become a contentious international trade issue.

In some local and regional markets, however, some producers are developing an interest in cultivating labels of origin unique to a particular geographic area, and are organizing their efforts under the American Origin Product Association (for more information, see: http://aopcentral.us/).

For more background information, see the USPTO's website (http://www.uspto.gov/ip/global/geographical/) and also CRS InFocus IF00016, Geographical Indications in U.S.-EU Trade Negotiations.

Among the reasons cited for the increasing popularity of local foods are perceived higher product quality and freshness of local food; a desire to provide social and political support for local farmers and the local economy; farmland preservation; concerns about environmental impacts and energy use and the perception that local foods are more environmentally friendly (limited use of chemicals, energy-based fertilizers, and pesticides); perceived better food safety given shorter supply chains; sense of social justice (perceived fairer labor prices and fair price for farmers); knowing the source of the product; a commitment to establishing closer connections between consumers and agricultural producers; and, generally, a response to concerns about industrialized commercial agriculture.[29] Important features include knowledge that production and distribution occur within a specific region, and that consumers are informed about the local nature of products, in some cases through personal communication with the farmers. Regardless of the distance the food travels from the production area to the consumer, many of these factors inherently influence consumer demand for products marketed and perceived to be "local." A desire to support farms using sustainable agriculture practices is often claimed as a motivation driving demand for local foods. However, just as there exists no definitive definition of "local"

---

[29] For example, S. Martinez, "Varied Interests Drive Growing Popularity of Local Foods," *Amber Waves*, USDA ERS, December 2010; S. Martinez et al., *Local Food Systems: Concepts, Impacts, and Issues*; Jennifer Jensen, "Local and Regional Food Systems for Rural Futures," Rural Policy Research Institute, November 2010; and Marne Coit, "Jumping on the Next Bandwagon: An Overview of the Policy and Legal Aspects of the Local Food Movement," National Agricultural Law Center, University of Arkansas School of Law, February 2009.

---

foods, much debate exists about what constitutes "sustainable agriculture." USDA's Sustainable Agriculture Research and Education (SARE) program has identified three pillars of sustainability: profit over the long term; stewardship of our nation's land, air, and water; and quality of life for farmers, ranchers, and their communities.[30] Another widely used definition also integrates three main goals—environmental health, economic profitability, and social and economic equity.[31]

Figure 3. Percent of Farms with Direct Sales, 2007

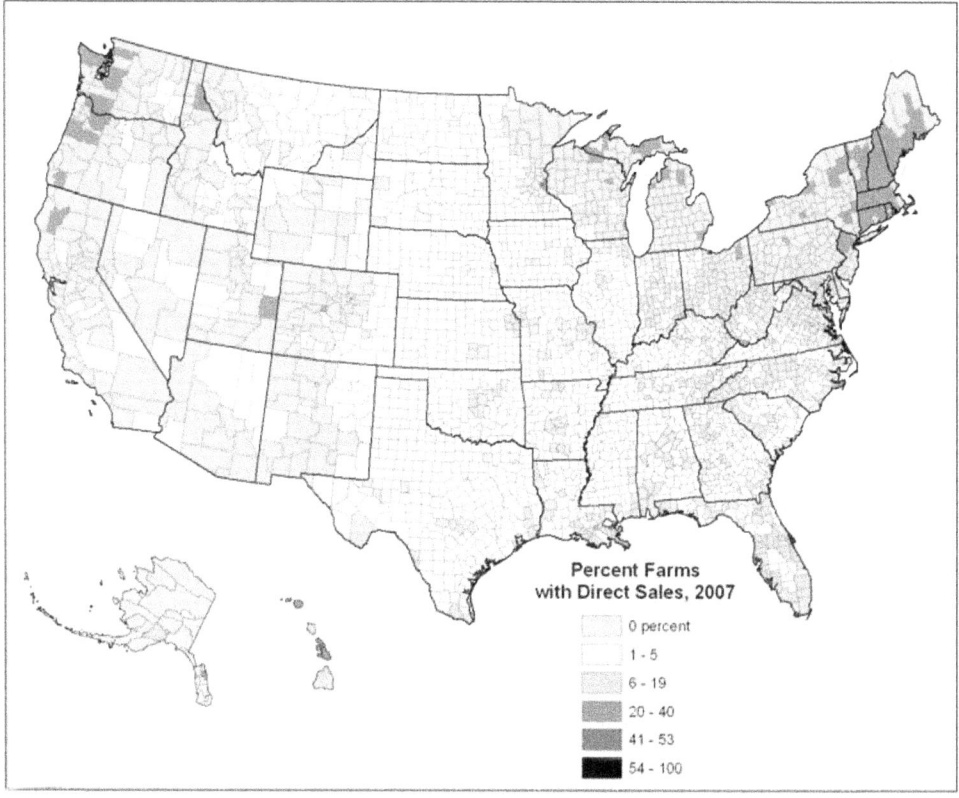

Source: CRS using USDA 2007 Census data.

A desire to support nearby small and medium-sized farms is also a motivation for consumers. USDA reports that small farms rely more on direct-to-consumer marketing channels (farmers' markets, on-farm sales, roadside stands, CSAs, etc.) as compared to larger farms. At small-sized farms (defined as farms with sales of less than $50,000), 88% of all sales are through direct-to-consumer channels, with 22% of sales made through intermediated market channels, including grocers, restaurants, and regional distributors (**Figure 4**). This compares with larger farms (sales of more than $250,000), where 40% of all sales were through intermediated channels. Consumer support could potentially help small businesses address some of the perceived challenges for marketing locally sourced foods. For example, USDA and others report that business barriers to market entry and expansion in local food markets include capacity constraints for small farms; lack of distribution systems for moving local food into mainstream markets; lack of resources for

---

[30] USDA SARE, "What Is Sustainable Agriculture?" http://www.sare.org/.

[31] University of California Sustainable Agriculture Research and Education Program (UC-SAREP), "What is Sustainable Agriculture?"

capital and infrastructure investments; and limited research, education, and training for marketing local food.[32] Other challenges facing producers include access to processing and packaging services; delivery procedures; consistency (volume and quality); uncertainties related to regulations that may affect local food production, such as food safety requirements; and need for traceback of foods to their origin. A 2011 study focused on beginning farmers cites challenges including lack of capital and access to credit and land, and cites as "valuable" programs such as apprenticeships, local partnerships, and CSAs.[33]

Figure 4. Reliance on Direct-to-Consumer Marketing

(small versus larger farms, share of annual sales)

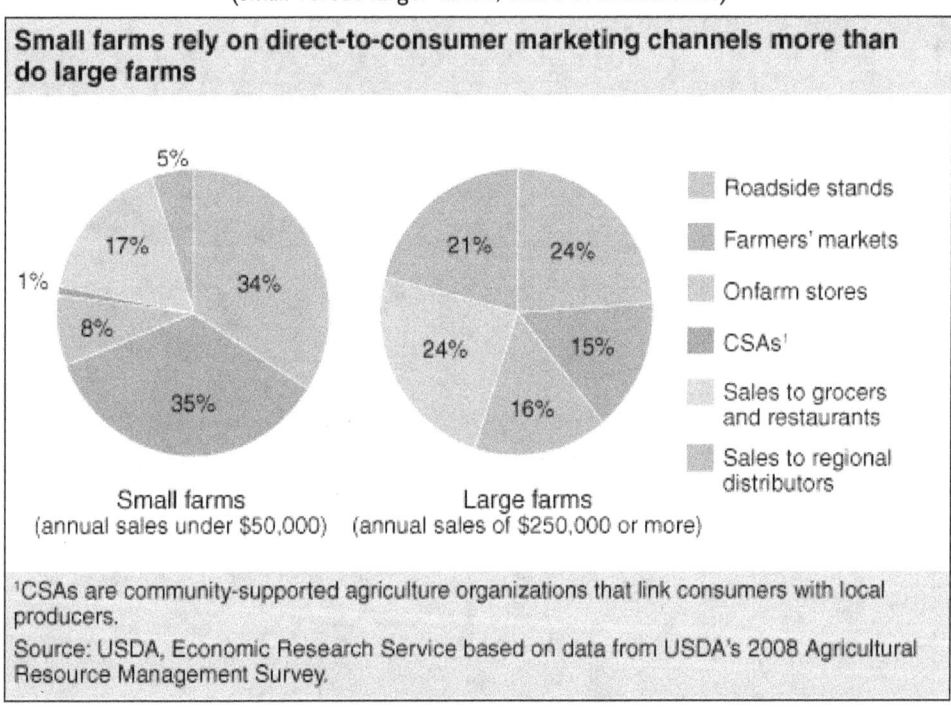

Small farms rely on direct-to-consumer marketing channels more than do large farms

Roadside stands
Farmers' markets
Onfarm stores
CSAs[1]
Sales to grocers and restaurants
Sales to regional distributors

Small farms
(annual sales under $50,000)

Large farms
(annual sales of $250,000 or more)

[1]CSAs are community-supported agriculture organizations that link consumers with local producers.
Source: USDA, Economic Research Service based on data from USDA's 2008 Agricultural Resource Management Survey.

Source: : S. Low and S. Vogel, "Local Foods Marketing Channels Encompass a Wide Range of Producers," *Amber Waves*, December 2011.

A study released in 2013 indicates that surveyed consumers believe purchasing locally sourced foods helps local economies (66%); delivers a broader and better assortment of products (60%); provides healthier alternatives (45%); improves the carbon footprint (19%); and increases natural or organic production (19%).[34] Among other study findings: about 30% of those surveyed said they would switch stores if their preferred store does not carry local foods, and indicated that their main source for local food is local farmers' markets and farm stores.

---

[32] See, for example: S. Martinez, et al., *Local Food Systems: Concepts, Impacts, and Issues*; American Farmland Trust, *Think Globally, Eat Locally: San Francisco Foodshed Assessment*, 2008; L. Day-Farnsworth, et al., "Scaling Up: Meeting the Demand for Local Food," December 2009; and R. King, "Can Local Go Mainstream?" C-FARE webinar, April 12, 2011.

[33] National Young Farmer's Coalition, *Building a Future With Farmers: Challenges Faced by Young, American Farmers and a National Strategy to Help Them Succeed*, November 2011.

[34] A. T. Kearney, "Buying into the Local Food Movement," 2013. Online survey of 1,300 U.S. respondents.

Option for Increasing Access to Fresh Foods in "Food Deserts"

Some groups advocate an increased role for local food systems to help address concerns about lack of consumer access to healthy, nutritious foods within certain low-income or underserved communities, such as in "food deserts." The 2008 farm bill defined a "food desert" as an "area in the United States with limited access to affordable and nutritious food, particularly such an area composed of predominantly lower-income neighborhoods and communities." (P.L. 110-246, Title VI, §7527). The Centers for Disease Control and Prevention (CDC) further clarified these areas as lacking "access to affordable fruits, vegetables, whole grains, low-fat milk, and other foods that make up the full range of a healthy diet."

A 2009 USDA report to Congress reported that of all U.S. households, 2.3 million households (2%) live more than 1 mile from a supermarket and do not have access to a vehicle; and an additional 3.4 million households (3%) live between one-half and 1 mile away and do not have access to a vehicle.

Other USDA data show where food deserts are located in the United States based on indicators of access and proximity to grocery stores, such as the share of residents that are low-income households without a car that live a certain distance from a supermarket or large grocery store. For mapping purposes, USDA defines a food desert as a low-income census tract where a substantial number or share of residents has low access to a supermarket or large grocery store. A "low-income community" has either (1) a poverty rate of 20% or higher, or (2) a median family income at or below 80% of the area's median family income. A "low-access community" has at least 500 people and/or at least 33% of the census tract's population must reside more than one mile from a supermarket or large grocery store (for rural census tracts, the distance is more than 10 miles).

Policy options identified to address food deserts include offering incentives (such as tax credits) to attract grocery stores to urban and rural communities; developing other retail outlets, such as farmers' markets, public markets, cooperatives, farm stands, CSAs, and mobile vendors; improving transportation and distribution networks; increasing stocks of fresh foods at neighborhood stores; and encouraging growing food locally through backyard and community gardens, as well as urban farms.

Additional information: CDC, "A Look Inside Food Deserts," http://www.cdc.gov/features/fooddeserts/. Also USDA, "Food Access Research Atlas" (http://www.ers.usda.gov/data/fooddesert) and USDA, ERS, *Access to Affordable and Nutritious Food: Measuring and Understanding Food Deserts and Their Consequences*, Report to Congress, April 2009.

Among the types of benefits cited by advocates of local food systems are increased and more stable farm incomes; increased jobs and wealth retention in local economies; improved access to fresh produce; enhanced accountability and choice; reduced vulnerability to contamination and food safety concerns, given the smaller distribution range of foods; diversified and sustainable production; and reduced energy use from reduced transportation (fewer "food miles") and reduced contributions to climate change.[35] Some of these claimed benefits have been disputed. In addition to raising questions about the general assumption that "local" is inherently good, other criticisms leveled against "local" include lowered productivity and inefficient use of resources in food production; questions about ecological sustainability and community effects; and concerns about food quality and food safety.[36] USDA reported that few academic studies demonstrate how local food markets may affect the economic development, health, or environmental quality of communities. Results from these limited available studies have indicated that expanding local food systems in a community can increase employment and income in that community; however, evidence is insufficient to determine whether local food availability improves diet quality or food

---

[35] See, for example, M. Anderson, "The Case for Local and Regional Food Marketing. Issue Brief for Farm & Food Policy Project," 2007, http://www.farmandfoodproject.org.

[36] See, for example, Brandon Born and Mark Purcell, "Avoiding the Local Trap," *Journal of Planning Education and Research*, 26: 195-207, 2006.

---

security or whether localized production results in a reduction of overall energy use or in greenhouse gas emissions.[37]

Estimated Number of Urban and Metropolitan Farms

An estimated 15% to 30% of the world's food supply is grown in urban areas.[38] Urban agriculture may include crops grown in backyards, city lots, or community gardens, or crops grown using hydroponic (or soil-less) systems, as well as livestock grazing in parks and feedlots. Food grown in urban areas may be "planted on private or public property including vacant lots, city parks, churchyards, schoolyards, and rooftops and on land owned individually, by a community group, institution, municipality, land trust, or other entity."[39] Urban agriculture is characterized as being produced in close proximity to where it is sold and consumed. Some noted objectives of urban agriculture include community and economic development; improved access to fresh, locally produced food; transformation of vacant urban property and collection and reuse of organic waste and rainwater; and education, organization, and employment of local residents. Several major cities have educational and apprentice programs geared to urban agriculture.[40]

"Urban farms" are generally larger-scale, more intensive operations managed by an organization or private enterprise to grow food for sale at retail stores, farmers' markets, and food fairs, or for field-to-direct-sales to consumers, food processors, and cottage food makers (home kitchens).[41] There are no compiled USDA data specific to farms located in urbanized areas in the United States. (For USDA data collection purposes, a "farm" is any place from which $1,000 or more of agricultural products were produced and sold, or normally would have been sold, during the year.) Limited USDA data and information are available on farms located in U.S. metropolitan (metro) areas, which cover a larger geographical area than urbanized areas.[42] (The U.S. Census Bureau defines an urbanized area (UA) as having 50,000 or more people.[43] Metropolitan areas are defined as a county or group of counties with an urban population of at least 50,000 people, plus any outlying counties that are economically connected to the central counties by communities.)[44]

USDA reports that, in 2007, there were about 859,300 metropolitan farms in the United States, accounting for about 40% of all U.S. farms and about 40% ($115.7 billion) of the total value of U.S. agricultural production.[45] Metropolitan farms are reported to have a different product mix

---

[37] S. Martinez, et al., *Local Food Systems: Concepts, Impacts, and Issues.*

[38] J. Smit, A. Ratta, and J. Nasr (Eds.), *Urban agriculture: food, jobs and sustainable cities*, Habitat II Series, United Nations Development Programme, 2001 edition; and USDA, "Urban Agriculture," http://afsic nal.usda.gov/.

[39] PolicyLink, "Urban Agriculture and Community Gardens, Why Use It?

[40] See http://justfood.org/farmschoolnyc (New York); http://www.growingpower.org/youth_education htm and http://start2farm.gov/programs/training-beginner-farmers-chicagos-urban-agriculture-community (Chicago, Milwaukee); and http://www.ecoffshoots.org/farmers/pgcc/ (Washington DC, Marlyand).

[41] See Maryland Department of Planning, *Planning for the Food System*, September 2012; USDA, "Urban Agriculture: List of References and Resource Guide 2000;" and PolicyLink, "Urban Agriculture and Community Gardens."

[42] U.S. Census Bureau maps comparing metropolitan and urbanized areas: "Combined Statistical Areas of the United States and Puerto Rico, December 2009" and "Urbanized Areas and also Urban Clusters: 2010" (http://www.census.gov).

[43] U.S. Census Bureau, "Urban and Rural Classification." Urban Clusters (UCs) are defined as having at least 2,500 and less than 50,000 people. "Rural" encompasses all population, housing, and territory not within an urban area.

[44] U.S. Census Bureau, "2010 Census Urban and Rural Classification and Urban Area Criteria."

[45] R. Hoppe and D. E. Banker, *Structure and Finances of U.S. Farms: Family Farm Report*, 2010 Edition, July 2010. The U.S. Census Bureau defines a "rural area" as open countryside with settlements and fewer than 2,500 inhabitants.

---

than farms in non-metro areas, and consist of mostly high-value crops, such as fruits and vegetables, and also livestock and dairy products. Tracking changes in agricultural production in metro areas over time is complicated by the fact that the number of counties classified as metropolitan has been increasing due to growing urbanization.

Information specific to farms in U.S. urbanized areas is more limited and available only to the extent that it is compiled by some states and localities.[46] The research institute PolicyLink highlights selected urban farms and projects in California, Illinois, Kansas, Ohio, Pennsylvania, Louisiana, New York, Massachusetts, Michigan, Washington, and Wisconsin, among other states, and also Puerto Rico.[47] Another study provides case studies of urban agriculture communities in Chicago; Cleveland; Detroit; Kansas City, Kansas and Missouri; Milwaukee; Minneapolis; New Orleans; Philadelphia; and Seattle and King County, Washington; as well as cities in Canada.[48]

To date, no comprehensive nationwide study exists of the number of urban agriculture sites in the United States. However, some studies provide estimates of the number of all urban agriculture sites—including urban farms—in certain cities and localities. For example, a 2012 study of the possible number of urban agriculture sites (including community gardens, vacant lot gardens, urban farms, school gardens, and home food gardens) in Chicago estimated that there were 4,648 urban agriculture sites with a production area of about 65 acres. Residential gardens and single-plot gardens on vacant lots accounted for about three-fourths of the total.[49] Of the 1,236 community gardens in Chicago, the study estimated that only 13% were producing food.

Studies of urban agriculture in New York indicate that there are more than 700 farms and gardens throughout the city's five boroughs that grow food (including urban farms, schoolyards, grounds of public housing developments, community gardens, and public parks).[50] A study of the Greater Philadelphia food system reports that there are more than 45,000 farms in the region's foodshed, which encompasses a 100-mile radius that extends from the center city of Philadelphia to 70 counties in five states, including Pennsylvania, New Jersey, Delaware, Maryland, and New York.[51] Other inventories indicate about 500 urban agriculture sites in Oakland, California, and about 300 sites in Portland, OR.[52] One county in Cleveland is estimated to have about 225 community gardens, with a combined space of about 56 acres, which is said to provide for about 1.5% of the county's produce.[53]

Other data compiled by USDA provide information on beginning farmers and ranchers, and cover all U.S. farms and not only farms in urban or metro areas, or farms that participate in local or

---

[46] In 2013, New York University, Pennsylvania State University, and the National Center for Appropriate Technology announced efforts to conduct a nationwide survey of urban and peri-urban farms.

[47] PolicyLink, "Urban Agriculture and Community Gardens, Why Use It?"

[48] K. Hodgson, et al., *Urban Agriculture, Growing Healthy, Sustainable Places*, APA Planning Advisory Service, 2011.

[49] "Finding Chicago's Food Gardens With Google Earth," *ScienceDaily*, January 3, 2013. The original study: J. R. Taylor and S. Taylor Lovell, "Mapping public and private spaces of urban agriculture in Chicago through the analysis of high-resolution aerial images in Google Earth," *Landscape and Urban Planning*, 108(1): 57.

[50] For example, K. Ackerman, et al., *The Potential for Urban Agriculture in New York City*, Earth Institute/Columbia University, [no date]. Jerome Chou, et al., *Five Borough Farm: Seeding the Future of Urban Agriculture in New York City*, Design Trust for Public Space/Added Value, [no date].

[51] Delaware Valley Regional Planning Commission, "Fact Sheet: Philadelphia's Food System," June 13, 2010.

[52] K. Hodgson, et al., *Urban Agriculture, Growing Healthy, Sustainable Places*, APA Planning Advisory Service, 2011.

[53] "Urban Agriculture Movement Blossoms in Cleveland," *NextGeneration*, Fall 2011.

regional food systems.[54] These data indicate that beginning farmers and ranchers accounted for about 22% of all U.S farms and ranches, and about 10% of all production in 2011. Compared to established farms, beginning farms and ranches tend to have lower average farm income and work more off-farm, and are also less likely to specialize in grain and row crop production, or participate in federal direct payment programs.

Types of Businesses and Operations

Data and information are available on the types of businesses engaged in local food systems, including farms that sell direct-to-consumer through farmers' markets, roadside stands, on-farm stores, CSAs, or other types of on-farm sales such as Internet or mail order sales, pick-your-own or "U-Pick" operations, cottage food makers, mobile markets, and also agritourism or other types of on-farm recreational activities.[55] Other forms of local food markets may include foods produced in community gardens or school gardens, urban farms (and rooftop farms and gardens), community kitchens, or small-scale food processing and decentralized root cellars. Following is a review of some of these types of direct-to-consumer marketing and other forms of local operations. Products sold through these outlets may include fresh foods, processed foods (such as honey, syrups, beef jerky, and homemade jellies, jams, and pickled products), and certain non-edible products such as nursery crops, cut flowers, and wool and other fiber products.

Locally produced foods may also pass through an intermediary, such as a restaurant, government institution, grocery store, or other retail channel. Food sales to farm-to-school programs may be direct from the farm or through an intermediary. Food hubs and market aggregators, along with kitchen incubators and mobile slaughter units, may be employed in distribution and/or processing within these marketing channels. Some of these types of food outlets are also reviewed.

Farmers' Markets

Farmers' markets are among several forms of direct farmer marketing, which also include farm and roadside stands, CSAs, pick-your-own farms, and direct sales to schools. More than 8,100 farmers' markets operated in 2014, up from about 6,100 in 2010, 2,700 in 1998, and 1,800 markets in 1994 (**Figure 5**).[56] **Figure 6** shows the number of farmers' markets, by county, in 2010.[57] In 2010, states with the most farmers' markets were California, New York, Illinois, Michigan, Iowa, Massachusetts, Ohio, Wisconsin, Pennsylvania, and North Carolina.[58] An estimated 1,225 farmers' markets operate during winter, mostly in New York, California, Pennsylvania, North Carolina, Ohio, Maryland, and Florida.[59]

---

[54] M. Ahearn, "Beginning Farmers and Ranchers at a Glance," Economic Brief No. (EB-22), January 2013, USDA.

[55] Ibid. Also: Cornell University, "Discovering the Food System, A Primer on Community Food Systems: Linking Food, Nutrition and Agriculture." For information on agritourism, see D. Brown and R. Reeder, "Agritourism Offers Opportunities for Farm Operators," *Amber Waves*, February 2008; and USDA's fact sheet, "Agricultural Diversification," http://www.agcensus.usda.gov.

[56] USDA, AMS, "Farmers' Market Growth: 1994-2011." Reflects updated USDA data.

[57] Original data are at USDA, http://ers.usda.gov/foodatlas/downloadData htm.

[58] USDA National Farmers' Market Directory is at http://apps.ams.usda.gov/FarmersMarkets.

[59] "Winter Farmers' Markets Expand to More than 1,200 Locations," *Agri-Pulse*, December 16, 2011.

Figure 5. National Count of U.S. Farmers' Markets Directory Listings

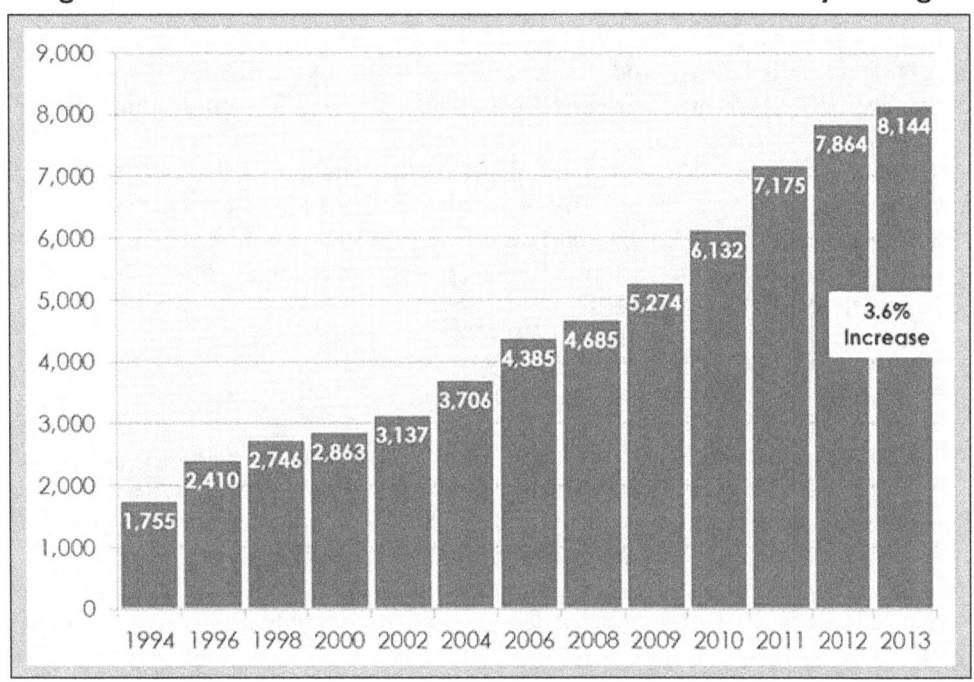

Source: USDA/AMS, "Farmers' Markets and Local Food Marketing," http://www.ams.usda.gov.

Figure 6. Number of Farmers' Markets, by County, 2010

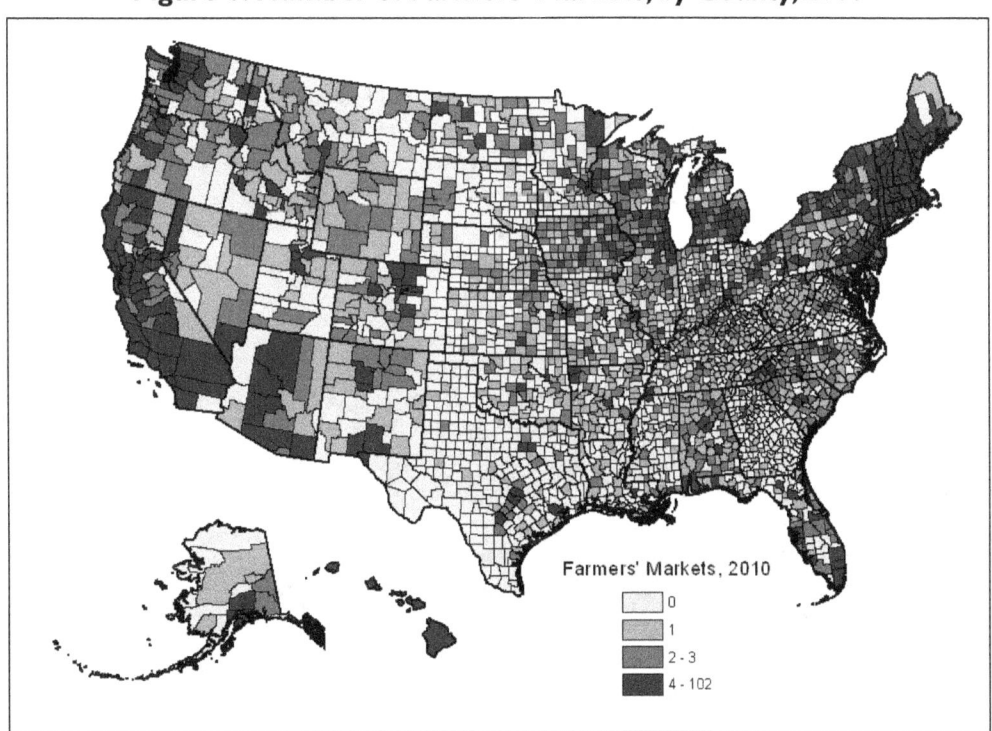

Source: CRS using USDA data for 2010.

USDA reported that total farmers' market sales were estimated to have exceeded $1 billion in 2009.[60] Products sold at farmers' markets include conventionally produced farm products and so-called natural and locally labeled products, as well as organically certified products[61] and other specially labeled products such as hormone- or antibiotic-free and free-range animal products.

USDA reported an average of about 30 vendors per market, suggesting that perhaps more than 120,000 farmers were selling at farmers' markets.[62] Previous estimates from USDA reported that 66,700 farmers were selling at farmers' markets, many of whom relied on such markets as their sole outlet.[63] USDA programs supporting farmers' markets are highlighted in **Table 2** and discussed in more detail in the **Appendix** of this report.

Farm-to-School Programs

Farm-to-school programs broadly refer to "efforts to serve regionally and locally produced food in school cafeterias," with a focus on enhancing child nutrition and providing healthier meals as part of the National School Lunch Program (NSLP) and other child nutrition programs.[64] The goals of these efforts include increasing fruit and vegetable consumption among students, supporting local farmers and rural communities, and providing nutrition and agriculture education to school districts and farmers.[65] School garden programs also build on this concept. Among the other goals of farm-to-school programs are those highlighted by the National Farm to School Network, connecting schools (K-12) and local farms with the objectives of serving healthy meals in school cafeterias, improving student nutrition, providing agriculture, health and nutrition education opportunities, and supporting local and regional farmers.[66] USDA's broader agency activities may also include other farm-to-institution activities involving hospitals or correctional facilities. USDA programs supporting farm-to-school programs are highlighted in **Table 2** and are discussed in more detail in the **Appendix** of this report.

USDA began its efforts "to connect farms to the school meal programs" in the late 1990s, as part of pilot projects in California and Florida, followed by other agency-wide initiatives in the early 2000s.[67] These efforts were reinforced by Congress as part of subsequent reauthorizations of child nutrition legislation, including the Healthy, Hunger-Free Kids Act of 2010 (P.L. 111-296).[68] During the 2011-2012 school year, the National Farm to School Network reports that more than 38,600 school (about 43% of all U.S. school) participated in more than 2,000 farm-to-school

---

[60] AMS, "Farmers Market Program Fact Sheet;" and AMS, *National Farmers' Market Manager Survey*, May 2009.

[61] Only a small percentage of certified organic products are direct marketed, according to studies cited by L. Lev and L. Gwin, "Filling in the Gaps: Eight Things to Recognize about Farm-Direct Marketing."

[62] USDA, AMS, *National Farmers' Market Manager Survey*, May 2009.

[63] USDA, AMS, *U.S. Farmers' Markets 2000: A Study of Emerging Trends*, May 2002.

[64] USDA, National Agriculture Library's (NAL) Alternative Farming Systems Information Center (AFSIC), "Farm to School," http://www.nal.usda.gov/afsic/. Child nutrition programs include the National School Lunch Program, School Breakfast Program, Child and Adult Care Food Program, Summer Food Service Program, Special Milk Program, and the Fresh Fruit and Vegetable Program.

[65] USDA, FNS, "Farm to School," http://www fns.usda.gov/farmtoschool/fact-sheets.

[66] National Farm to School Network, http://www.farmtoschool.org. See also B. Bellows, et al., "Bringing Local Food to Local Institutions," NCAT publication, October 2003; and UC-SAREP, "Direct Marketing to Schools," July 2002.

[67] AFSIC, "Farm to School;" and National Farm to School Network, "Farm to School Chronology."

[68] For more information on this law, see CRS Report R41354, *Child Nutrition and WIC Reauthorization: P.L. 111-296*.

---

programs across all 50 states, using local farms as food suppliers for school meals programs.[69] This compares to an initial two programs in the 1996-1997 school year, and an estimated 400 in 2004 and 1,000 in 2007. An estimated $355 million was spent on local food purchases through these programs.[70] Nearly 20% of school districts have guidelines for purchasing locally grown produce.[71] USDA's website provides information on national and regional farm-to-school programs and other resource guides.[72]

Figure 7 shows the number of farm-to-school program, by county, in 2009. According to the National Farm to School Network, states with the greatest number of schools participating in farm-to-school programs are North Carolina, Kentucky, Texas, Connecticut, Massachusetts, California, Florida, and Vermont. (Farm-to-school programs may provide a model for other related types of programs, such as farm-to-institution and farm-to-WIC[73] programs.)[74]

Figure 7. Number of Farm-to-School Programs, 2009

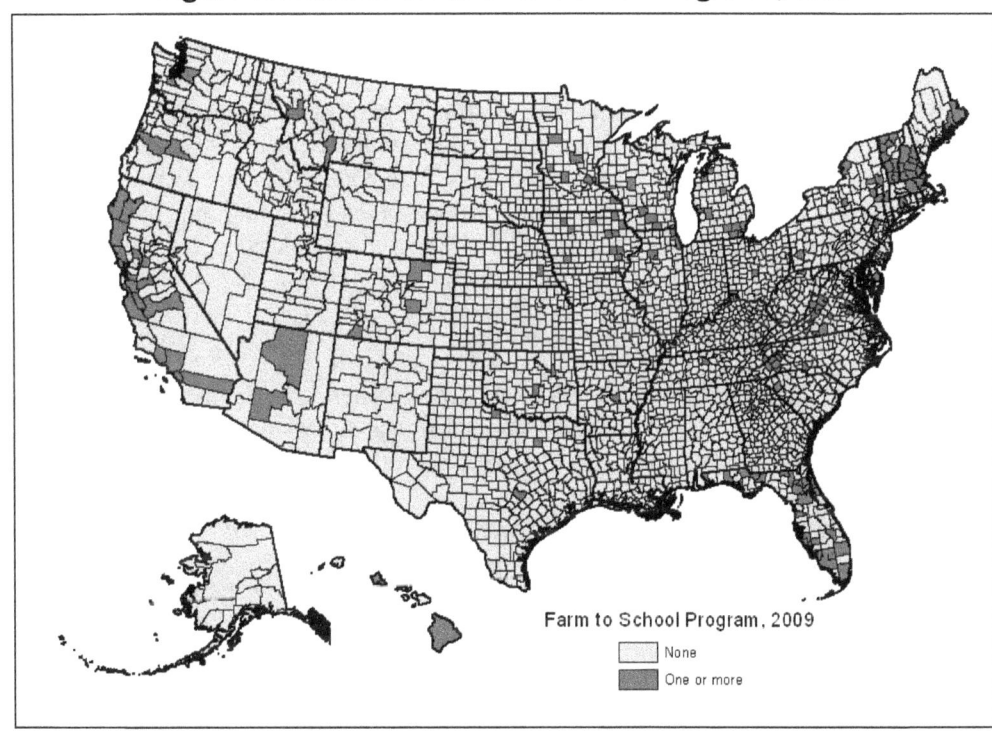

Source: CRS using 2009 USDA data. Original data are at USDA, http://www.ers.usda.gov/data-products/food-access-research-atlas.aspx.

---

[69] National Farm to School Network, http://www.farmtoschool.org.

[70] Ibid.

[71] Information from the National Farm to School Network data and USDA-sponsored School Nutrition and Dietary Assessment Survey, as cited in S. Martinez, et al., *Local Food Systems: Concepts, Impacts, and Issues*.

[72] AFSIC, "Farm to School," and Farm to School Network, http://www.farmtoschool.org/files/publications_277.pdf.

[73] WIC refers to the Special Supplemental Nutrition Program for Women, Infants, and Children (WIC). L. Kaiser et al., "UC Cooperative Extension explores a farm-to-WIC program," *California Agriculture*, January-March 2012.

[74] The Center for Agriculture and Food Systems (CAFS) and National Farm to School Network (NFSN), *State Farm to School Legislative Survey*, http://www.farmtoschool.org/policy.

Community-Supported Agriculture (CSA)

CSAs provide a way for consumers to buy local, seasonal food directly from a farmer. CSAs "directly link local residents and nearby farmers, eliminating 'the middleman' and increasing the benefits to both the farmer and the consumer."[75] In a CSA, a farmer or community garden grows food for a group of local residents—members, shareholders, or subscribers—who pledge support to a farm at the beginning of each year by agreeing to cover the farm's expected costs and risks. In return, the members receive shares of the farm's production during the growing season. The farmers receive an initial cash investment to finance their operation as well as a higher sales percentage because the crop is marketed and delivered directly to the consumer. The CSA model was first developed in Japan in the 1960s (known as "teikei," or "food with the farmer's face on it"), and was widely adopted in Europe in the 1970s.[76]

More than 1,400 CSAs were in operation in the United States in 2010.[77] The first U.S. CSA started in 1985 at Indian Line Farm in Massachusetts. By 2001 an estimated 400 CSAs were in operation, rising to 1,144 CSAs in 2005. USDA estimates that 12,549 farms marketed products through a CSA in 2007.[78] Overall, compared to a total of about 2 million farms, farms that sell through CSAs comprise less than 1% of all U.S. farming operations. California, Texas, and Kentucky were the leading states with farms that sold through a CSA in 2007. Other states with more than 400 farms selling through CSAs were Iowa, Michigan, Missouri, Washington, Ohio, Wisconsin, and North Carolina. USDA's website provides a listing of national, state, and regional organizations related to CSAs.[79] **Figure 8** shows the farms with CSA sales, by state, in 2007.

Community Gardens and School Gardens

The American Community Garden Association (ACGA) defines a community garden as "any piece of land gardened by a group of people," whether it is in an urban, suburban, or rural area, or whether it grows food, such as vegetables, or flowers and other horticultural products. It may be composed of a single community plot, or can be a collection of many individual plots. These gardens may be located at a school, hospital, or in a neighborhood, or may be dedicated to "urban agriculture" in a city-like setting where the produce is grown often for sale at market.[80] There are an estimated 18,000 community gardens throughout the United States.[81] Of these, about 1,600 gardens are recognized as People's Gardens under USDA's initiative and related programs (see "People's Garden Initiative," below).[82] A precise count of the number of school gardens in the

---

[75] USDA, Rural Development, "Community Supported Agriculture," http://www.rurdev.usda.gov/rbs/CDP-TN20.PDF.

[76] AFSIC (http://www.nal.usda.gov/afsic/) and USDA, Rural Development, "Community Supported Agriculture."

[77] Information from the National Center for Appropriate Technology (NCAT), cited in S. Martinez, et al., *Local Food Systems: Concepts, Impacts, and Issues.*

[78] USDA, 2007 *Agriculture Census*, Table 44 ("Selected Practices"). Data on marketed volumes is not available.

[79] See USDA (http://www.nal.usda.gov/afsic/pubs/csa/csaorgs.shtml) and Agricultural Marketing Resource Center.

[80] ACGA, "What Is a Community Garden?" http://www.communitygarden.org/learn/. Web-based locators are available at the NGA, http://www.garden.org/public_gardens; also http://acga.localharvest.org/. Also see AFSIC, "Community Gardening," http://www.nal.usda.gov/afsic/; NCAT Sustainable Agriculture Project, "Urban and Community Agriculture," http://attra.ncat.org/attra-pub/local_food/urban_ag.html; and K. Adam, "Community Garden," NCAT publication, IP376, January 2011.

[81] ACGA, "FAQs," http://communitygarden.org/learn/faq.php. A map of locations is at ACGA, http://acga.localharvest.org/. Data not available for Alaska and Hawaii.

[82] USDA, "Find a Garden in Your Area," http://www.usda.gov/wps/portal/usda/usdahome?navid= PEOPLES_GARDEN.

United States is not available; however, the National Gardening Association's "School Garden Registry" has information on several thousand school gardens across the nation (searchable by city, state, or name).[83] Other reports indicate that California alone had more than 2,000 school gardens in 2007.[84]

Figure 8. Farms with CSAs, by State, 2007

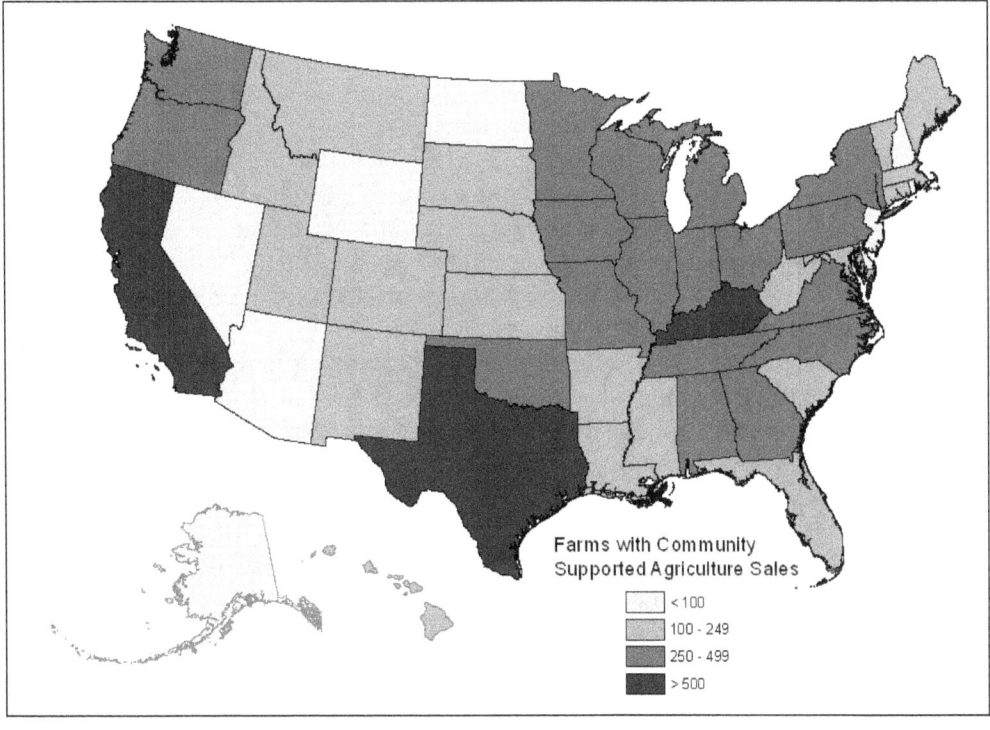

Source: CRS using USDA 2007 Census data.

The National Gardening Association (NGA) estimates that about 42 million households (35% of all U.S. households) participated in food gardening in 2013, up from an estimated 36 million households in 2008.[85] Much of this increase is attributable to an increase in the number of urban households growing food, as well as the number of food gardeners, aged 18-34 years old, and households with children. An estimated 3 million households were growing food at a community garden, up from 1 million in 2008. In total, U.S. households spent $29.5 billion on their lawns and gardens last year, average about $350 per household annually.

Community gardens have been establishing linkages with urban farming efforts and with efforts to increase access to fresh foods within some low-income and underserved communities (or "food deserts"). The history of community gardens goes back more than 100 years, starting with subsistence vegetable farming on vacant lots in Detroit in the early 1900s and encompassing

---

[83] NGA, "School Garden Search," http://www.kidsgardening.org/groups/school-garden-search.

[84] E. Ozer, "The Effects of School Gardens on Students and School: Conceptualization and Considerations for Maximizing Healthy Development," *Health Education & Behavior*, Vol. 34 (6): 846-863), December 2007.

[85] NGA, *Garden to Table: A 5-Year Look at Food Gardening in America*, March 2014 (as reported in "Food Gardening In The U.S. At The Highest Levels In More Than A Decade According To New Report By The National Gardening Association," *PR Newswire*, April 2, 2014); and NGA, "The Impact of Home and Community Gardening In America," 2009. Food gardening includes growing vegetables, fruit, berries, and herbs.

"Liberty Gardens" and "Victory Gardens" during the first and second World Wars, among other urban gardening movements over the period.[86] Despite initial concerns by USDA that Victory Gardens were an inefficient use of available resources, during WWII the agency encouraged nearly 20 million home gardeners to plant food. By the end of the war, home gardeners were producing a reported 40% of the nations' produce. Today, in addition to gardens that grow produce for personal consumption, some "market gardens" also grow produce for sale or for donation, and are part of a growing interest in urban agriculture—both farms and gardens. Resources available to households that want to grow their own food include benefits under the Supplemental Nutrition Assistance Program (SNAP, formerly food stamps), which lists among eligible food items "seeds and plants which produce food for the household to eat."[87]

Many school gardens are said to be based on a model developed in the mid-1990s as part of the Edible Schoolyard Project, largely attributed to the efforts of Berkeley, CA, restaurant owner Alice Waters.[88] School gardens are now being integrated into some educational curricula to provide nutrition and science education while teaching children about plants and nature, and the importance of eating healthy, nutritious foods. A number of nonprofit organizations support school gardens and provide resources for classrooms.[89] FoodCorps, an independent nonprofit organization, places young leaders into limited-resource communities for one year of public service to work with local partners teaching kids about food and nutrition, engaging them in school gardens, and supporting local healthy food for public school cafeterias.[90] USDA also recently funded a pilot program to support school gardens in high-poverty schools. (For more information see the **Appendix** of this report.)

In addition, various groups support a range of education and youth empowerment/work programs, as well as small-scale urban agriculture initiatives in many cities, including Chicago, Detroit, Philadelphia, Cleveland, and New York.[91] Also, many large cities—including Washington, DC, Baltimore, New York, and San Francisco—are developing their own food policy task forces to address local food initiatives within their cities.[92]

Food Hubs and Market Aggregators

A food hub refers to a warehouse or similar facility that aggregates food and facilitates sales to wholesale customers or directly to consumers.[93] A produce packing house may also act as an aggregation facility that prepares and receives raw fruits and vegetables from farmers. Such

---

[86] "History of Urban Agriculture," http://sidewalksprouts.wordpress.com/history/; USDA, "Victory Garden Leader's Handbook," 1943; and Pennsylvania State Council of Defense, "Handbook of the Victory Garden Committee War Services," April 1944.

[87] USDA, "SNAP: Eligible Food Items," http://www fns.usda.gov/snap/retailers/eligible htm. Congress added this provision in the 1970s. See SNAPgardens.org, "History," http://www.snapgardens.org/history/.

[88] See Edible Schoolyard Project, http://edibleschoolyard.org/.

[89] A list of resources and organizations is available from Civil Eats (see "School Gardens Across the Nation, and a Resource List for Starting Your Own," at http://civileats.com/2010/01/19/school-gardens-across-the-nation/).

[90] FoodCorps, "FoodCorps Launches National Service Program," August 2011, http://www.foodcorps.org. Host sites include Arkansas, Arizona, Iowa, Maine, Massachusetts, Michigan, Mississippi, New Mexico, North Carolina, Oregon.

[91] See, for example, Policy Link, "Equitable Strategies for Growing Urban Agriculture" webinar.

[92] N. Shute, "Big-City Mayors Dig In to Food Policy," *The Salt*, National Public Radio, January 19, 2012.

[93] National Good Food Network, "The Business of Food Hubs: Planning Successful Regional Produce Aggregation Facilities," September 30, 2010, webinar (http://www.ngfn.org/resources/ngfn-cluster-calls/the-business-of-food-hubs).

---

aggregation points allow for "scaling up" of agricultural production from the farm to the marketplace, linking farmers to consumers.[94] Ideally, they are located near the farms they serve to better help farmers scale up and connect with consumers, wholesalers, retailers and grocery stores, restaurants, and food-service buyers such as schools or hospitals. (In addition, some states also have their own state-branded systems that may be accessible through their own online directory.) Most aggregators provide an online directory or virtual marketplace to link buyers and sellers. Many also provide assistance to participate in farm-to-school programs and other types of services, including agritourism. In some cases, a range of educational services, technical assistance, and outreach are provided, intended to advance agricultural entrepreneurship. Examples include on-the-ground farmer training, aggregation and distribution, capacity-building, curriculum development, and help with food safety certification, usually through linkages with state extension and university staff.[95]

USDA estimates that more than 170 food hubs operate in the United States, with large clusters located in the Midwest and Northeast.[96] One example is MarketMaker, an interactive database of food industry marketing and business data, which is intended to link food-producing farmers with buyers in the marketplace. The database contains more than half a million businesses, including more than 2,500 farmers' markets and nearly 1,000 agritourism businesses, as well as farmers, processors, wholesalers, buyers, and retailers. It spans 18 participating states[97] and the District of Columbia and covers nearly 900 general product categories. Based on information from the directory's expanded user profiles, up to 47% of those participating are farmers. A large share of those are fruit and vegetable growers. Other product categories include meat, fish, seafood, dairy products, wineries, and a range of specialty products. MarketMaker started in 2004 as a national partnership of land grant institutions and state departments of agriculture, and is maintained by University of Illinois.[98] It was initially funded through grants from the Illinois Council on Food and Agricultural Research (CFAR), a state-based grant program, and continues to be maintained through appropriated USDA research funding and various state-level resources.

Another regional aggregator is FoodHub, an online directory linking food buyers and sellers for a range of food products.[99] It also provides a forum for users to post food products and/or services that they wish to sell or buy, and covers more than 3,000 products. It currently has more than 2,500 members and operates in six states: Alaska, California, Idaho, and Montana, but mostly in Oregon and Washington State. Its membership consists of buyers (40%), sellers (38%), associates (19%), and distributors (3%). The site is intended to be both scale and production system-neutral, and is open to commercial buyers, independent producers, regional distributors, industry suppliers, farmers' markets, trade associations, nonprofits, and the media. FoodHub was initially started with funding from two USDA programs, the Specialty Crop Block Grant Program and the

---

[94] See, for example, hearing before the Senate Committee on Agriculture, Nutrition, and Forestry, "Healthy Food Initiatives, Local Production, and Nutrition," March 7, 2012. Comments by Jody Hardin, Hardin Farms.

[95] CRS communication with University of Illinois staff, September 15, 2011. An example includes the University of Kentucky's "MarketReady" training program, which helps small farmers and ranchers address the market development risks and relationship management as they develop relationships with buyers (http://www.uky.edu/fsic/marketready/).

[96] USDA, "USDA Identifies Infrastructure and Economic Opportunities for Regional Producers," Release No. 0170.11, April 19, 2011; and USDA blog, "USDA 2012 Agricultural Outlook Forum: Making Locally Grown Food More Available," January 25, 2012.

[97] Alabama, Arkansas, Colorado, Florida, Georgia, Illinois, Indiana, Iowa, Kentucky, Louisiana, Michigan, Mississippi, Nebraska, New York, Ohio, Pennsylvania, South Carolina, and Texas.

[98] MarketMaker, http://national marketmaker.uiuc.edu/.

[99] FoodHub is a project of the nonprofit Ecotrust (http://food-hub.org/).

Rural Business Enterprise Grant, and is supported by member fees. FoodHub provides additional resources and support for farm-to-school and farm-to-hospital programs as well as for school gardens and food banks, including guidance on getting started, finding funding, developing menus, and applying for grants. In 2010, FoodHub had more than 20 K-12 schools participating, including the Portland public school system, serving 20,000 meals per day.

Kitchen Incubators

A kitchen incubator (also culinary incubator, including shared-use commercial kitchens for rent) is a business that provides food preparation facilities to help a small start-up or home-based business produce a food product.[100] A kitchen incubator is often a fixed-location small food processing facility, serving as a resource for a new business (such as an early-stage catering, retail, or wholesale food business) that may not have the capital to invest in its own full-time licensed commercial kitchen (providing an alternative for cottage food makers and home kitchens).[101] Instead, the new business is able to rent shared space in a fully licensed commercial kitchen, which also helps it comply with federal and state food safety laws and requirements. There are reportedly more than 100 kitchen incubators nationwide.[102] The types of businesses that use kitchen incubators include start-up or home-based food producers, caterers, bakers, street vendors, and makers of specialty food items, such as condiments and candies, and also in some cases established food businesses.

Mobile Slaughter Units

A mobile (also modular) slaughter unit (MSU) is a self-contained USDA-inspected slaughter and meat processing facility that can travel from site to site and can be used by small-scale meat producers who may not have resources to transport animals to a distant slaughterhouse (often referred to using the French term, *abattoir*) or who may want to sell locally raised meat directly to local consumers or restaurants. MSUs provide a trained and licensed workforce, and are required to comply with necessary food safety, sanitation, hygiene, and waste management requirements. MSUs were also a response to increased consolidation in the meat and poultry industries, resulting in fewer slaughter facilities and a lack of USDA- or state-inspected establishments "available to small producers of livestock and poultry in some remote or sparsely populated areas."[103] MSUs are able to serve multiple small producers in areas where slaughter services might be unaffordable or unavailable. One of the first mobile USDA-inspected slaughter units started operation in the early 2000s in Washington State.[104]

---

[100] Culinary Incubator, "8 Things to Consider when Considering a Culinary Incubator," http://www.culinaryincubator.com/tenant_information_kitchen_rental.php. Also USDA, "Agriculture Deputy Secretary Celebrates Opening of a Non-Profit Pennsylvania Kitchen for Use by Food Entrepreneurs," June 17, 2011; National Business Incubation Association (http://www.nbia.org/). Includes early-stage catering, retail and wholesale food businesses. Differs from a community kitchen, where people share a common kitchen to prepare one food to share.

[101] USDA, "Urban Agriculture: An Abbreviated List of References and Resource Guide 2000," September 2000; and PolicyLink, "Urban Agriculture and Community Gardens," http://www.policylink.org/. Several states do have cottage food laws in place that allow for home processing (see "Cottage Food Law by States," http://cottagefoods.org/laws/).

[102] See databases at http://www.culinaryincubator.com/maps.php.

[103] USDA, "Mobile Slaughter Unit Compliance Guide," and USDA, "Slaughter Availability to Small Livestock and Poultry Producers—Maps," May 4, 2010.

[104] MSU, "State of the Art Mobile Processing Unit for Small Scale Producers," http://www.mobileslaughter.com/.

Federal Programs and Initiatives

Following is a discussion of existing federal programs administered by USDA and other agencies that potentially can support local food systems, as well as some of the Obama Administration's initiatives intended to support local food systems. Data are not available to determine the extent to which local producers and local food system providers are actively participating in these programs. A more comprehensive table and description of existing programs is included in the **Appendix** at the end of this report.

Selected USDA Programs

Many existing USDA assistance programs are available to all U.S. farmers, regardless of farm size or distance from markets. Federal programs that provide support to all U.S. producers—including local producers—cover a wide range of USDA programs contained within various titles of the 2014 farm bill (P.L. 113-79, Agricultural Act of 2014) and the most recent reauthorization of the child nutrition programs (P.L. 111-296).[105]

In the farm bill, an array of farm assistance programs that might be considered to support local food systems are contained within several titles: conservation (Title II); nutrition (Title IV); farm credit (Title V); research (Title VI); rural development (Title VII); horticulture (Title X); and disaster assistance (Title XI). (See selected farm bill titles in text box.) The 2010 child nutrition reauthorization includes additional food nutrition programs that might also be considered to support local food systems.

Within each farm bill title are many individual programs. Many of these are also highlighted by the Obama Administration as part of its "Know Your Farmer, Know Your Food" Initiative (discussed later). Among the USDA programs available for leveraging local and regional food production systems are:

- Marketing and promotion programs, such as the Specialty Crop Block Grant Program; Farmers' Market and Local Food Promotion Program; and Federal State Marketing Improvement Program.

- Business assistance programs, such as Value-Added Agricultural Product Market Development Grants; Beginning Farmer and Rancher Development Program; USDA's Microloan Program; Small Business Innovation Research; Agricultural Management Assistance; Community Outreach and Assistance Partnership Program; and Outreach and Assistance to Socially Disadvantaged Farmers and Ranchers.

- Rural and community development programs, such as Rural Cooperative Development Grants; Business and Industry (B&I) Guaranteed Loans; Community Facilities Program; Rural Business Enterprise Grants (RBEG); Rural Business Opportunity Grant (RBOG); and Rural Microentrepreneur Assistance Program.

---

[105] For information on the omnibus farm bill, see CRS Report R43076, *The 2014 Farm Bill (P.L. 113-79): Summary and Side-by-Side*. For information on the child nutrition reauthorization, see CRS Report R41354, *Child Nutrition and WIC Reauthorization: P.L. 111-296*.

- Research and cooperative extension programs, such as Sustainable Agriculture Research and Education programs.

- Nutrition and school-based programs, such as Farmers' Market Nutrition Programs; the Supplemental Nutrition Assistance Program (SNAP) at Farmers' Markets; USDA's Farm to School grant Program; School Gardens; commodity procurement through "DoD Fresh"; Healthy Food Financing Initiative; Community Food Projects. 2014 farm bill added new authorizations, including a pilot for schools purchases of fruits and vegetables in place of USDA purchases and the Food Insecurity Nutrition Incentive grant program.

The 2014 Farm Bill (P.L. 113-79): Functions and Major Issues, by Title

- **Title I, Commodity Programs:** Provides support for major commodity crops, including wheat, corn, soybeans, peanuts, rice, dairy, and sugar, as well as disaster assistance.

- **Title II, Conservation:** Encourages environmental stewardship of farmlands and improved management through land retirement and/or working lands programs.

- **Title III, Trade:** Provides support for U.S. agricultural export programs and international food assistance programs.

- **Title IV, Nutrition:** Provides nutrition assistance for low-income households through programs including the Supplemental Nutrition Assistance Program (SNAP).

- **Title V, Credit:** Supports federal direct and guaranteed loans to farmers and ranchers.

- **Title VI, Rural Development:** Supports business and community programs and coordination activities with other local, state, and federal programs.

- **Title VII, Research, Extension, and Related Matters:** Supports agricultural research and extension programs.

- **Title VIII, Forestry:** Supports forestry management programs run by USDA's Forest Service.

- **Title IX, Energy:** Supports the development of farm and community renewable energy systems through various programs, including grants and loan guarantees.

- **Title X, Horticulture:** Supports the production of specialty crops—fruits, vegetables, tree nuts, and floriculture and ornamental products—through a range of initiatives.

- **Title XI, Crop Insurance:** Enhances coverage of the permanently authorized federal crop insurance program.

- **Title XII, Miscellaneous:** Other types of programs and assistance not covered in other bill titles, including provisions affecting livestock and poultry production.

Other types of USDA programs not listed here include selected USDA research and cooperative extension programs, as well as USDA conservation programs, among others (see **Table 2**). Many of these programs have been identified by the National Sustainable Agriculture Coalition (NSAC) in its *Guide to USDA Funding for Local and Regional Food Systems*.[106] These selected programs are administered by various USDA agencies, including the Agricultural Marketing Service

---

[106] NSAC, *Guide to USDA Funding for Local and Regional Food Systems*. April 2010.

(AMS), Rural Development (RD), Risk Management Agency (RMA), National Institute of Food and Agriculture (NIFA), Agricultural Research Service (ARS), Natural Resources Conservation Service (NRCS), and Food and Nutrition Service (FNS).

Many community and rural development groups and small-farm advocacy organizations have promoted initiatives intended to support the development of local food markets by building on the existing USDA programs to create new market opportunities for small and medium-sized farms.[107]

The **Appendix** to this report provides a brief summary of selected federal programs that may be considered to provide support to local food systems. This is not a comprehensive listing of all the possible programs that are administered by each USDA agency, particularly of research and conservation programs that generally support all U.S. farmers, including producers of local food. In addition to various federal efforts, a number of states, communities, and other entities have spearheaded initiatives that support local food systems. This report does not cover these efforts, since there is limited aggregate information on them.

Data are not available to determine the share of available funding for the programs in the **Appendix** used to support local and regional food systems, compared to all other types of farming systems. For many of the programs highlighted, most indications suggest that the share used to support local food systems is likely very small. Among USDA's farm support programs, only a few target direct support to local food systems, as discussed in the following section.

Loans for Local Food Producers

The 2008 farm bill amended an existing USDA Rural Development agency loan program—the Business and Industry (B&I) loan and loan guarantee program—to provide that 5% of the available funding support local and regional food production. Eligible recipients under the provision include "individuals, cooperatives, cooperative organizations, businesses, and other entities to establish and facilitate enterprises that process, distribute, aggregate, store, and market locally or regionally produced agricultural food products to support community development and farm and ranch income."[108] The 2008 farm bill defined an eligible "locally or regionally produced agricultural food product" as "any agricultural food product that is raised, produced, and distributed in ... the locality or region in which the final product is marketed, so that the total distance that the product is transported is less than 400 miles from the origin of the product"; or "any agricultural food product that is raised, produced, and distributed in ... the State in which the product is produced." With obligations for the B&I loan program averaging more than $1 billion annually, this means that available funding for loans directed to local and regional food producers is more than $50 million each year. Additional information is in the **Appendix**.

In addition, in 2013, USDA announced it had created a new microloan program within the existing direct farm operating loan program, using its regulatory prerogative, to "better serve the unique financial operating needs of beginning, niche and the smallest of family farm operations."[109] The microloan program simplifies and expedites the application process, and adds

---

[107] See, for example, NSAC, "Guide to USDA Funding for Local and Regional Food Systems," April 2010.

[108] P.L. 110-246, §6015 (Locally or Regionally Produced Agricultural Food Products).

[109] FSA, "Microloan Fact Sheet," January 2013, http://fsa.usda.gov/Internet/FSA_File/microloans_eng_jan2013.pdf. Also see 78 *Federal Register* 12, 3828-3836, January 17, 2013. The program is administered through FSA's Operating (continued...)

---

flexibility for meeting loan eligibility and security requirements. The maximum microloan size is $35,000, and the loans can be used for all approved operating expenses as authorized by the FSA Operating Loan Program. The 2014 farm bill (P.L. 113-79, § 5106) authorized a similar program to allow USDA to make or guarantee loans or to provide related services. Additional information is in the **Appendix**.

Local Food Purchases in Child Nutrition Programs

While specific grant programs may support farm-to-school work, it is possible—within the framework of procurement law—for schools and child-care institutions to use per-meal cash reimbursements (from participating in the USDA FNS child nutrition programs) to purchase foods from local and regional food systems. The 2008 farm bill amended existing child nutrition programs to include language that would encourage school food authorities to purchase fresh produce and would require USDA to allow school food authorities receiving child nutrition funds under programs to use a geographic preference.[110] The law required USDA "to encourage institutions receiving funds under the National School Lunch Act and the Child Nutrition Act to purchase unprocessed agricultural products, both locally grown and locally raised, to the maximum extent practicable and appropriate."[111] This provision is structured as a preference and does not require states and school food authorities to include geographic preference in their procurement. Because geographic preference still operates within the framework of existing procurement law, schools can face barriers to purchasing when a local product is not the lowest-cost bid. USDA has provided guidance, suggesting that applying geographic preference points may enable a local product to still win a contract.[112]

In addition to the cash reimbursements that states and schools receive, they also receive federal assistance in the form of USDA commodity foods.[113] The 2008 farm bill revised but retained a requirement that $50 million per year of commodity procurement funds be used to purchase fresh fruits and vegetables for schools.[114] USDA uses a partnership with the Department of Defense (DOD) to procure and distribute fresh produce to schools; this program offers fruits and vegetables labeled as "local" for schools to select.[115] The 2014 farm bill this funding requirement and added a requirement for USDA to carry out a pilot project that would allow up to eight states

---

(...continued)

Loan Program (Farm and Rural Development Act, as amended, P.L. 92-419, 7 U.S.C. 1942 (CFDA# 10.406)). For other information see CRS Report RS21977, *Agricultural Credit: Institutions and Issues*.

[110] P.L. 110-246, §4302 (Purchases of Locally Produced Foods), amending §9(j) of the Richard B. Russell National School Lunch Act (42 U.S.C. 1758(j)).

[111] Ibid.

[112] See http://www.fns.usda.gov/cnd/Governance/Policy-Memos/2011/SP18-2011_os.pdf (questions 5, 6, and 7).

[113] For more information on the purchase of USDA Commodity Foods, see CRS Report RL34081, *Farm and Food Support Under USDA's Section 32 Program*. For information on food distribution to schools, see USDA, FNS "Frequently Asked Questions" http://www.fns.usda.gov/fdd/programs/schcnp/schcnp_faqs htm/.

[114] P.L. 110-246, §4404(c).

[115] USDA and DoD websites communicate that the procurement program's advantages include "greater buying power, consistent deliveries, emphasis on high quality, a large variety of produce items including pre-cuts and *locally grown*, and an easy-to-use ordering website with funds tracking." USDA-FNS, "DoD Fresh Fruit and Vegetable Program," http://www.fns.usda.gov/fdd/programs/dod/DOD_FreshFruitandVegetableProgram2011.pdf (emphasis added).

to use this funding for their own local sourcing of fresh fruits and vegetables to schools.[116] More information is in the **Appendix**.

Grants for Farm-to-School Programs

The 2010 child nutrition reauthorization (P.L. 111-296) amended existing child nutrition programs to establish mandatory funding of $5 million per year for competitive grants that would assist schools and nonprofit entities in establishing farm-to-school programs that improve a school's access to locally produced foods.[117] Grants are not to exceed $100,000 and will require 75% matching funds. Grants may be used for training, supporting operations, planning, purchasing equipment, developing school gardens, developing partnerships, and implementing farm-to-school programs. The 2014 farm bill also created a Food and Agriculture Service Learning Program to increase capacity for food, garden, and nutrition education and to complement the work of the farm-to-school grants; $25 million in funding is authorized to be appropriated. Additional information is provided in the **Appendix**.

Other USDA Actions

For FY2010, USDA established by administrative notice that each state must fund at least one project that supports the USDA's "Know Your Farmer, Know Your Food" initiative (discussed below), as part of the agency's Rural Housing Service Strategic Plan.[118] This notice applied to available funding for USDA's Community Facilities programs, which include loans and grants for water and environmental projects, and community facilities projects.[119] The types of eligible projects include food banks (e.g., certain building purchase, construction, and renovations, equipment and vehicle purchases); school cafeterias (e.g., certain equipment, renovations, central processing/distribution centers); farmers' markets that primarily sell fruits and vegetables (e.g., certain new construction, building purchases, and renovations); community gardens (e.g., real estate purchases, water source access and infrastructure); and community kitchens that provide classes for families to learn how to prepare healthy meals (e.g., certain renovations, equipment, and new construction).

Examples of Non-USDA Programs

Aside from USDA, resources that can be used to support local and regional food systems exist at other U.S. federal agencies.

For example, the U.S. Department of the Treasury's New Markets Tax Credit (NMTC) is a non-refundable tax credit intended to encourage private capital investment in eligible, impoverished, low-income communities. These include communities that have limited access to fresh and

---

[116] P.L. 113-79, §4202.

[117] P.L. 111-296, §243 (Access to Local Foods: Farm to School Program), amending §18 of the Richard B. Russell National School Lunch Act (42 U.S.C. 1758(j)). In addition, appropriations are authorized "such sums as are necessary for each of fiscal years 2011 through 2015."

[118] Letter to State Directors, Rural Development, from Tammye Treviño, Administrator, Housing and Community Facilities Programs, regarding the Community Facilities Funding for Local and Regional Food Systems Projects and Know Your Farmer Know Your Food Initiative, June 2010.

[119] USDA, "Community Facilities Loans and Grants," http://www.rurdev.usda.gov/HCF_CF html.

nutritious foods ("food deserts"). The program was authorized by the Community Renewal Tax Relief Act of 2000 (P.L. 106-554) to stimulate investment in low-income communities. NMTCs are allocated by the Community Development Financial Institutions (CDFI) fund, a bureau within U.S. Treasury, under a competitive application process.[120]

Treasury's CDFI Fund is also part of what has been a multi-agency Administration initiative to support the development of healthy, fresh food retail in areas lacking such options, the Healthy Food Financing Initiative (HFFI). Since FY2011, the Administration has pursued food retail development through pre-existing authorities and programs at Treasury, HHS, and USDA, but focused these authorities on increasing access to healthy, affordable food in "food deserts." These programs are discussed in the next section.

Potentially helpful programs also are available in other federal agencies, including the Department of Housing and Urban Development; the Commerce Department's Economic Development Administration; and the Small Business Administration. In addition, most states are active in direct marketing and farmers' market activities, usually through their state departments of agriculture.[121]

Administration Initiatives

USDA's *Strategic Plan FY2010-2015* outlines the core strategic goals and the primary objectives for the department.[122] Enhancing rural prosperity, supporting sustainable and competitive agricultural systems, and increasing access to nutritious food are among these goals and objectives. Many of these same priorities are reflected in the department's various initiatives, such as the "Know Your Farmer, Know Your Food" Initiative, the Regional Innovation Initiative, and the Healthy Food Financing Initiative.

"Know Your Farmer, Know Your Food" Initiative

"Know Your Farmer, Know Your Food" is a USDA-wide management initiative that was launched by USDA in September 2009 to "begin a national conversation to help develop local and regional food systems and spur economic opportunity."[123] The initiative was designed to eliminate organizational barriers between existing USDA programs and promote enhanced collaboration among staff, leveraging existing USDA activities and programs, and thereby "marshalling resources from across USDA to help create the link between local production and local consumption."[124] It is not a stand-alone program and does not have its own budget;[125] instead, it is a departmental initiative, and not connected to a specific office or subagency. This is

---

[120] For more information, CDFI's website (http://www.cdfifund.gov/what_we_do/programs_id.asp?programID=5). See also CRS Report RL34402, *New Markets Tax Credit: An Introduction*.

[121] USDA and farmers' market websites provide state contacts (http://www.ams.usda.gov/AMSv1.0/FMPP). Other information is available from the National Association of State Departments of Agriculture (http://www.nasda.org/).

[122] USDA, *Strategic Plan FY2010-2015*.

[123] USDA, "USDA Launches 'Know Your Farmer, Know Your Food' Initiative to Connect Consumers with Local Producers to Create New Economic Opportunities for Communities," September 15, 2009.

[124] USDA, "Our Mission," http://www.usda.gov/wps/portal/usda/knowyourfarmer?navtype=KYF&navid= KYF_MISSION; and USDA, AMS, "Regional Food Hubs: Linking Producers to New Markets," May 2011.

[125] Letter to Senators McCain, Roberts, and Chambliss from USDA Secretary Vilsack, April 30, 2010.

---

done by highlighting various existing programs within USDA that are available to support local farmers; strengthen rural communities; promote healthy eating; protect natural resources; and provide grants, loans, and support.[126] Linking local production with local consumption of farm products also is one of the primary goals of USDA's Regional Innovation Initiative (see below).

Among the programs mentioned for leveraging local and regional food production systems are marketing and promotion programs; rural business and community development programs; and selected USDA research and cooperative extension programs.[127] In response to demand for farm-to-school activities, certain USDA nutrition and domestic food programs, such as the farm-to-school and some fresh fruit and vegetable programs, also have been associated with the initiative. Since its launch, USDA has announced funding for various projects under these and other programs identified as promoting local-scale sustainable operations.[128]

USDA's website lists many other existing agency programs that might be available to provide assistance to eligible farming businesses. Accordingly, the initiative spans existing, mostly long-standing programs within most USDA's agencies, including Rural Development (RD), Research, Education and Economics (REE), Farm Service Agency (FSA), and Agricultural Marketing Service (AMS).[129]

USDA's websites provide additional information on the initiative, including (1) information on financial and technical assistance resources from USDA for local food enterprises (http://www.usda.gov/knowyourfarmer); and (2) information on USDA resources for community-level projects and a mapping of funded projects (http://www.usda.gov/kyfcompass).

In April 2013, USDA Secretary Tom Vilsack announced the agency's intentions to institutionalize its "Know Your Farmer, Know Your Food" Initiative by making it a permanent part of activities throughout USDA.[130]

Criticism of USDA's Initiative

Previously, some in Congress have challenged USDA's "Know Your Farmer, Know Your Food" initiative. In April 2010, three Senators wrote a letter to USDA Secretary Vilsack expressing concerns about the initiative. The letter stated: "This spending doesn't appear geared toward

---

[126] USDA, http://www.usda.gov/wps/portal/usda/knowyourfarmer?navid=KNOWYOURFARMER; see also USDA memos at http://www.usda.gov/wps/portal/usda/knowyourfarmer?navtype=KYF&navid=KYF_GRANTS.

[127] See USDA, "Our Mission"; and NSAC, "Guide to USDA Funding for Local and Regional Food Systems."

[128] For example, USDA's initial press release announced the following efforts under this initiative: collaborative outreach and assistance programs to socially disadvantaged and underserved farmers; implementation of a new voluntary cooperative program for state-inspected establishments to ship meat and poultry in interstate commerce; and grants to help local business cooperatives, and also the Northwest Food Processors Association.

[129] See "USDA Deputy Secretary Kathleen Merrigan's Memos," http://www.usda.gov/wps/portal/usda/knowyourfarmer?navtype=KYF&navid=KYF_GRANTS. These include "Memo on Rural Development Programs," August 26, 2009; "Memo on Research, Education and Economics," October 29, 2009; "Memo on Farm Service Agency," June 17, 2010; and "Memo on Agricultural Marketing Service," July 20, 2010. USDA's Regional Innovation Initiative also spans several USDA agencies, including agencies from USDA's Rural Development, Marketing and Regulatory Programs, and Natural Resources and Environment mission areas. USDA, "USDA Launches 'Know Your Farmer, Know Your Food' Initiative to Connect Consumers with Local Producers to Create New Economic Opportunities for Communities," September 15, 2011, Release No. 0440.09.

[130] "Vilsack: USDA to 'institutionalize' Know Your Farmer, Know Your Food," *The Hagstrom Report*, April 19, 2013.

---

conventional farmers who produce the vast majority of our nation's food supply, but is instead aimed at small, hobbyist and organic producers whose customers generally consist of affluent patrons at urban farmers' markets," among other concerns regarding USDA's promotion and prioritization of local food systems. The letter also requested evidence of USDA's congressional authority to spend money for "Know Your Farmer, Know Your Food" and a full itemized accounting of all spending under the initiative.[131] In response, USDA clarified that the initiative

> does not have any budgetary or programmatic authority.... Rather, it is a communications mechanism to further enable our existing programs to better meet their goals and serve constituents as defined in the respective authorizing legislation and regulations. While there are no programs under the initiative, since September 2009 a number of our program funding announcements have included a reference to 'Know Your Farmer, Know Your Food.'[132]

USDA also asserts that "none of these programs are providing preference to local and regional food system projects, except as provided for in their existing regulatory rules or legislative authority."[133] According to USDA, there are only two such statutory cases—a 5% set-aside established in the 2008 farm bill for rural development Business and Industry (B&I) loans and an allowance for schools to make local purchases under the Department of Defense Fresh Fruit and Vegetable Program (DoD Fresh).[134] In addition, USDA issues an administrative notice requiring that the agency's Rural Housing and Community Facilities Program provide "that each state must fund at least one project" supporting the initiative in FY2010 only. (See "Other USDA Actions.")

The initiative remains controversial. Following extensive House floor debate on the FY2012 Agriculture appropriations bill, the House-passed bill included a number of provisions restricting funding for selected USDA programs that fund this initiative and also other local and regional food production projects.[135] The Senate bill did not put restrictions on the use of USDA funds to support USDA's initiative. The enacted FY2012 Agriculture Appropriations Act (P.L. 112-55) did not specifically address this initiative, but the joint explanatory statement required USDA to report any travel related to the initiative, including the agenda and the cost of such travel, and to include justification for this initiative in its FY2013 budget request.[136] USDA was also required to submit a report to Congress on the impacts of the initiative during the previous two years (within 90 days of enactment).

Following USDA's submission of its report, Senator Pat Roberts, ranking Member of the Senate Agriculture Committee, expressed concerns about the department's initiative, since most food consumed in the United States is not locally grown, and questioned whether it might result in redundancy, given the number of USDA agencies involved in this initiative. He also raised concerns about "where do we get the most bang for the taxpayer buck?"[137] Later, at a March 2012

---

[131] Letter to USDA Secretary Vilsack from Senators McCain, Roberts, and Chambliss, April 27, 2010.

[132] Letter to Senators McCain, Roberts, and Chambliss from USDA Secretary Vilsack, April 30, 2010.

[133] Ibid.

[134] CRS communication with USDA staff, June 14, 2011. It is not known how much schools spent on local purchases under USDA's farm to school programs in recent years.

[135] H.R. 2112, House-reported version, §750. For more information, see CRS Report R41964, *Agriculture and Related Agencies: FY2012 Appropriations.*

[136] H.Rept. 112-284, p. 190 (*Congressional Record*, November 14, 2011, pp. H7433-7576).

[137] Senator Roberts press release, "Senator Roberts: USDA Report Shows Misuse of Taxpayer Dollars," February 29, 2012. Also see S. Wyant, "Sen. Roberts: USDA's Know Your Farmer, Know Your Food" isn't 'steeped in reality," *Agri-Pulse*, February 29, 2012.

---

hearing before the committee, Ranking Member Roberts questioned whether locally produced foods should be considered better than conventionally produced foods, and whether this pits farmers against each other.[138] He also questioned whether local markets should receive public assistance, given growing consumer demand for locally produced products in the marketplace.

USDA's Report to Congress

As required by the FY2102 enacted appropriations, in February 2012, USDA released its report to Congress along with the so-called Know Your Farmer, Know Your Food "Compass," an interactive web-based document and map highlighting USDA support for local and regional food projects.[139] The Compass's map shows USDA-supported projects and programs related to local and regional food systems from 2009 to 2012, mapped by selected theme (e.g., Local Meat; Farm to Institution; Infrastructure; Stewardship; Healthy Food Access; Marketing/Promotion, etc.).[140]

The report provides a compilation of available information, highlighting different types of local and regional food system projects, along with case studies. The report highlights that USDA has identified at least 27 programs—mostly grant, loan, and loan guarantee programs—administered by nine different USDA agencies supporting local and regional food producers and businesses.[141] The report also claims that operations with local sales result in additional farm employment, citing previous estimates from USDA based on fruit and vegetable farms. These estimates show that operations with local food sales generate, on average, 13 operator full-time equivalents (FTEs) per $1 million in sales, compared to operations without local sales that generate 3 FTEs per $1 million in sales.[142] The report claims that nearly all U.S. states and congressional districts benefit from local and regional food systems in some way. The initial USDA launch of the report was followed by a webinar further explaining the Compass and how USDA believes that local and regional food systems benefit the U.S. economy.[143] Other recent and related USDA publications include a report on the distribution practices of eight producer networks and their partners distributing locally or regionally grown food to retail and food-service customers.[144]

Regional Innovation Initiative

The "Regional Innovation Initiative" (RII) was launched in 2010 and funding was requested as part of the Administration's FY2011 and FY2012 funding requests to "focus on the planning and coordination of USDA and other sources of assistance for rural communities."[145] These five rural

---

[138] Comments from Senator Pat Roberts, hearing before the Senate Committee Agriculture on Agriculture, Nutrition, and Forestry, "Healthy Food Initiatives, Local Production, and Nutrition," March 7, 2012.

[139] "USDA Unveils the Know Your Farmer, Know Your Food Compass," Release No. 0072.12, February 29, 2012.

[140] "Know Your Farmer, Know Your Food Compass Map," http://www.usda.gov/maps/maps/kyfcompassmap htm.

[141] USDA, "Know Your Farmer, Know Your Food," page 27, http://www.usda.gov/documents/KYFCompass.pdf.

[142] S. Low and S. Vogel, *Direct and Intermediated Marketing of Local Foods in the United States*, ERR-128, USDA Economic Research Service (ERS), November 2011, p. 12.

[143] USDA, "Media Advisory: USDA to Continue National Conversation on Local and Regional Food Systems," Media Advisory No. 5060.12, March 5, 2012.

[144] USDA, AMS, "Moving Food Along the Value Chain: Innovations in Regional Food Distribution," March 2012. Also see USDA, "New Study Explores Innovation and Opportunities for Diverse Local Food Distributors," Release No. 0096.12, March 16, 2012.

[145] USDA, "FY2011 Budget Summary and Annual Performance Plan," http://www.obpa.usda.gov/.

development pillars are also outlined in USDA's *Strategic Plan FY2010-2015*.[146] The initiative is intended as the agency's "different direction as it relates to rural development," and spans five rural development pillars: rural broadband; biofuels and biobased products; linking local production and consumption of farm products; ecosystem markets to pay producers for sequestering carbon; and forest restoration and private land conservation.[147] The Administration's FY2012 budget proposal endorsed "strategic leveraging of existing resources to strengthen rural communities" through the initiative. However, Congress provided no funding to USDA for the initiative in the enacted FY2012 Agriculture appropriations.[148]

Although funding was not provided, Congress did address this initiative during the appropriations debate. The House-passed Agriculture appropriations report stated that the committee is "unable to provide any funding or authorization for the initiative as requests for additional information on the specific purpose, need, and plans for the initiative have gone unanswered" and directed USDA not to spend any of its funding for the Rural Community Development Initiative (RCDI) on the initiative without Congress's approval.[149] The Senate bill did not put restrictions on the use of USDA funds to support USDA's initiative. The enacted FY2012 appropriations law also did not specifically address this initiative.

Healthy Food Financing Initiative

The "Healthy Food Financing Initiative" (HFFI) was launched in 2010 and funding has requested as part of the Administration's FY2011-FY2015 funding requests to "support local and regional efforts to increase access to healthy foods, particularly for the development of grocery stores and other healthy food retailers in urban and rural food deserts and other underserved areas."[150] HFFI is based on the Pennsylvania Fresh Food Financing Initiative and similar efforts in other states to attract fresh-food retail investment in underserved communities through one-time grants and loan financing.[151]

Since the beginning of HFFI, it has included programs at USDA, HHS, and/or the Treasury, ; funding amounts and agencies have varied depending on annual appropriations. Programs making up the HFFI have been:

- Treasury's CDFI Fund allocates the New Market Tax Credits (discussed earlier) and also administers related Healthy Food Financing Initiative grants. The Fund reported that it awarded 10 HFFI awards (totaling $22 million) in FY2013, on top

---

[146] USDA, *Strategic Plan FY2010-2015*, http://www.ocfo.usda.gov/usdasp/sp2010/sp2010.pdf.

[147] Jon Harsch, "Sec. Vilsack proposes 'Regional Innovation Initiative' for rural America," *Agri-Pulse*, March 3, 2010. For more about rural development programs generally, see CRS Report RL31837, *An Overview of USDA Rural Development Programs*.

[148] See CRS Report R41964, *Agriculture and Related Agencies: FY2012 Appropriations*.

[149] H.Rept. 112-101.

[150] USDA, "FY2011 Budget Summary and Annual Performance Plan," http://www.obpa.usda.gov/.

[151] CDFI Fund, Healthy Food Retail Financing At Work: *Pennsylvania Fresh Food Financing Initiative*, September 30, 2011, http://www.cdfifund.gov/. Illinois and New York have similar policies, along with Detroit, New York City, New Orleans, and Washington, DC. For other information, see comments from John Weidman, The Food Trust, at a hearing before the Senate Committee Agriculture on Agriculture, Nutrition, and Forestry, "Healthy Food Initiatives, Local Production, and Nutrition," March 7, 2012.

of the more than $172 million in Financial Assistance and Technical Assistance awards through its core CDFI program.[152]

- HHS's Community and Economic Development (CED) program provides competitive discretionary grants authorized by the Community Services Block Grant Act (P.L. 105-285).[153] An existing program that predated the Administration's HFFI, the portion of the CED program dedicated to HFFI since FY2011. The CED program support projects that finance grocery stores, farmers' markets, and other retail outlets for fresh nutritious food.[154] The program provides funding for projects designed to address the healthy food access needs of low-income individuals and families through the creation of employment and business opportunities. Among its goals are to revitalize communities and to eliminate food deserts. Eligible uses include startup or expansion of businesses or physical or commercial activities; capital expenditures such as purchases of equipment or real property; allowable operating expenses; and loans or equity investments. Eligible applicants include private, nonprofit organizations that are community development corporations (CDCs), including faith-based organizations and tribal organizations.

- USDA's Rural Business Services had supported businesses through its existing loan, grant, and technical assistance programs. This HFFI-related authority was last funded in FY2011.[155]

The 2014 farm bill (P.L. 113-79, § 4206) has the potential to change the administration of HFFI in FY2015 or subsequent years, depending in part on appropriations action. This provision authorizes up to $125 million to be appropriated for HFFI at USDA, to remain available until expended. Under this provision, USDA is authorized to approve a community development financial institution as "national fund manager" that would administer these funds by supporting food retail projects that "expand or preserve access" to staple foods listed in the law and accept SNAP benefits. The FY2015 President's Budget requests funding for USDA – citing the 2014 farm bill's authority – and CDFI, but none for HHS.[156]

People's Garden Initiative

In February 2009, USDA announced its plans to develop a People's Garden at USDA facilities.[157] Since then, USDA has funded a number of other initiatives and programs to help communities

---

[152] Community Development Financial Institutions Fund, "Treasury Awards Over $172 Million To Organizations Serving Low-Income Communities," September 24, 2013, at http://www.cdfifund.gov/news_events/CDFI-2013-40-TREASURY_AWARDS_OVER_$172_MILLION_TO_ORGANIZATIONS_SERVING_LOW-INCOME_COMMUNITIES.asp.

[153] For more information, CED's website (http://www.acf.hhs.gov/programs/ocs/programs/ced).

[154] Ibid. Also, Debra Tropp, "Support of Local Food Initiatives," USDA AMS, October 2010.

[155] Among the stated reasons for not funding USDA's HFFI program was that HFFI "has yet to prove that any expenditures made for this initiative have been effective" in meeting the goal of ensuring that more people have access to nutritious foods. H.Rept. 112-284. See also CRS Report R41964, *Agriculture and Related Agencies: FY2012 Appropriations*.

[156] FY2015 President's Budget requested $13 million for USDA loans and grants under the authority of P.L. 113-79, Section 4206, along with $35 million for CDFI Fund technical assistance and financial assistance. No funds were requested for HHS. See Office of Management, The Appendix, FY2015 Budget for selected agencies.

[157] USDA, "Vilsack Establishes The People's Garden Project on Bicentennial of Lincoln's Birth," February 12, 2009.

---

establish community and school gardens nationwide "through collaborative efforts."[158] To date, USDA claims that more than 1,600 gardens are recognized as People's Gardens, involving more than 750 partnering organization.[159] These efforts often mirror similar activities promoted through First Lady Michelle Obama's *Let's Move!* initiative.[160]

In FY2010, USDA provided $1 million in funding for the People's Garden School Pilot Program.[161] This pilot program was authorized by Congress in the 2008 farm bill, which provided for grants to high-poverty schools to promote healthy food education and hands-on gardening in the school curriculum. The program is administered by FNS. The FY2010 funding was awarded to Washington State University, which is expected to serve an estimated 2,800 students attending 70 elementary schools in Washington, New York, Iowa, and Arkansas.[162]

In FY2011, USDA provided approximately $725,000 in grants for its People's Garden Grant Program, administered by NIFA.[163] Activities under this program were authorized in the National Agricultural Research, Extension, and Teaching Policy Act (P.L. 95-113) to facilitate the initial investment needed to create produce, recreation, and/or wildlife gardens in urban and rural areas, and provide opportunities for science-based non-formal education. In 2011, projects were funded in Alaska, Arizona, California, Colorado, Connecticut, Hawaii, Maryland, Michigan, and Ohio.[164]

Reports from USDA indicate other People's Garden efforts and volunteerism within other USDA agencies, including NRCS and FSA.[165] For FY2015, funding for "Visitor Center/People's Garden" is reported at $0.9 million.[166] For additional information, see "School Gardens" in the **Appendix**.

Congressional Actions

Legislative Options

Authorization for many of the selected programs highlighted in this report are contained within periodic farm bills or within the most recent reauthorization of the child nutrition programs.

---

[158] USDA, People's Garden Initiative FAQ, http://www.usda.gov/documents/Common_Questions_feb2012.pdf.

[159] To qualify, gardens must (1) benefit the community, (2) be collaborative, and (3) incorporate sustainable practices. USDA, "Find a Garden in Your Area," http://www.usda.gov/wps/portal/usda/usdahome?navid=PEOPLES_GARDEN.

[160] See, for example, *Let's Move!* press releases: "School Garden Concept Plan Revealed to Students at Powell Elementary School," March 14, 2011; and "Let's Move! to grow more Community Gardens," April 28, 2011, http://www.letsmove.gov/blog/.

[161] USDA's budget justification for FY2011, http://www.obpa.usda.gov/30fns2011notes.pdf. See p. 30-10.

[162] USDA, "USDA Announces Funding to Expand School Community Gardens and Garden-Based Learning Opportunities," August 25, 2010.

[163] NIFA, "People's Garden Grant Program," http://www.csrees.usda.gov/fo/peoplesgardengrantprogram.cfm.

[164] NIFA, "Abstracts of Funded Projects," http://www.csrees.usda.gov/fo/peoplesgardengrantprogram.cfm.

[165] USDA blog, "The People's Garden Initiative Celebrates 3 Years of Growth," February 17, 2012.

[166] USDA's budget justification for FY2015, http://www.obpa.usda.gov/04da2015notes.pdf. See p. 4-3.

Farm Bill Reauthorization

Omnibus farm bills govern U.S. agricultural and food programs, covering a wide range of programs and provisions, and are reviewed and renewed roughly every five years. Although many of these policies can be and sometimes are modified through freestanding authorizing legislation or as part of other laws, the omnibus, multi-year farm bill provides a predictable opportunity for policymakers to address agricultural and food issues more comprehensively. The Agricultural Act of 2014 (P.L. 113-79) is the most recent omnibus farm bill, and was enacted into law in February 2014. It succeeded the Food, Conservation, and Energy Act of 2008 (P.L. 110-246, (2014 farm bill") is the most recent omnibus farm bill, and replaces the 2008 farm bill (P.L. 110-246, The Food, Conservation, and Energy Act of 2008).[167]

In recent years, a diverse mix of community and rural development groups and small-farm advocacy organizations have actively promoted initiatives intended to support the development of local and regional food systems by reforming the existing farm support framework and building on the concept of direct farm-to-consumer marketing to create new economic opportunities for small and medium-sized farms. Some domestic food-related and public health organizations were promoting initiatives to improve access to healthy, nutritious foods for schools and underserved communities. The National Sustainable Agriculture Coalition (NSAC) actively advocated to reduce total farm bill spending through payment limits and other reforms, while increasing investments in certain perceived underfunded areas, such as support for new farmers, rural development, conservation, renewable energy, agricultural research, and new market development.[168] Other groups advocating for an increased role for local food systems in the farm bill are the Institute for Agriculture and Trade Policy (IATP),[169] Food & Water Watch,[170] and the Union for Concerned Scientists,[171] as well as several anti-hunger and community advocacy groups such as Feeding America,[172] the Community Food Security Coalition,[173] The Food Trust,[174] and Green for All,[175] among others.

In addition, some states, including California, submitted farm bill recommendations, seeking to promote specialty crop production to enhance fruit and vegetable production and to improve public health and nutrition, and also to revitalize local communities, support organic agriculture, and enhance the natural environment, among other goals.[176] Meanwhile some state and local groups, such as the Pennsylvania-based nonprofit organization The Food Trust, were promoting

---

[167] See CRS Report RS22131, *What Is the Farm Bill?* More detailed information see CRS Report R43076, *The 2014 Farm Bill (P.L. 113-79): Summary and Side-by-Side.*

[168] NSAC, *Farming for the Future: National Sustainable Agriculture Coalition Releases its 2012 Farm Bill Platform,* March 19, 2012, and "NSAC Releases Letter to the Super Committee and Farm Bill Budget Views," September 20. Also see NSAC's 2012 "Farm Bill Platform: Budget Chapter Background."

[169] IATP, "Everyone at the Table: Local Foods and the Farm Bill," March 28, 2012.

[170] Food & Water Watch, *Farm Bill 101,* January 2012, and "Rebuilding Local Food Systems," February, 2011.

[171] Union for Concerned Scientists, "Toward Healthy Food and Farms," February 2012.

[172] Feeding America, "Food Policy Forum: Opportunities to Combat Hunger and Improve Nutrition in the 2012 Farm Bill," February 14, 2012 (series of farm bill program presentations for congressional staff).

[173] Community Food Security Coalition, "Federal Policy Program," http://www.foodsecurity.org/policy html.

[174] The Food Trust, "The Food Trust Mission," http://www.thefoodtrust.org/php/about/OurMission.php.

[175] Green For All, *Green Jobs in a Sustainable Food System,* April 2011.

[176] California Department of Food and Agriculture (CDFA), "California and the Farm Bill: A Vision for Farming in the 21st Century."

---

expanded farmers' market programs and farm-to-school programs, as well as initiatives to reduce the number of food deserts nationwide.[177] These types of recommendations were proposed by a variety of other groups and think tanks.[178]

Child Nutrition Reauthorization

Child nutrition programs and the Special Supplemental Nutrition Program for Women, Infants, and Children (WIC) provide cash, commodity, and other assistance under three major federal laws: the Richard B. Russell National School Lunch Act (originally enacted as the National School Lunch Act in 1946), the Child Nutrition Act (originally enacted in 1966), and Section 32 of the Act of August 24, 1935 (7 U.S.C. §612c). Congress periodically reviews and reauthorizes expiring authorities under these laws. The most recent reauthorization of the child nutrition programs was in 2010, the Healthy, Hunger-free Kids Act of 2010 (P.L. 111-296).[179] In the 2008 farm bill, Congress expanded the Fresh Fruit and Vegetable (Snack) Program, amending the Richard B. Russell National School Lunch Act.[180]

Other Proposed Legislation

Several bills were introduced in the 112th and 113th Congress broadly addressing local and regional food systems. Some of the introduced bills represented comprehensive "marker bills" addressing provisions across multiple farm bill titles and recommending changes that would have provided additional directed support for local and regional food systems.[181] Some in Congress have expressed the need to change farm policies in ways that might also enhance support for local food systems and rural communities.[182]

The Senate Committee on Agriculture, Nutrition, and Forestry held a hearing, "Healthy Food Initiatives, Local Production, and Nutrition," in March 2012 addressing some of these issues.[183] Other House and Senate farm bill briefings were conducted on a variety of topics related to local and regional food systems.[184]

One of the more comprehensive marker bills introduced in the 112th and 113th Congress was the Local Farms, Food, and Jobs Acts of 2011 and 2013 (**H.R. 3286/S. 1773** (112th Congress) and **H.R. 1414/S. 679** (113th Congress); Pingree/Brown). These bills proposed comprehensive

---

[177] The Food Trust, "Farmers' Market Alliance" and "Bipartisan 'Healthy Food Financing' Bills Would Create Jobs and Cut Dietary Diseases," http://www.thefoodtrust.org.

[178] See, e.g., Harry A. Wallace Center, "Making Changes: Turning Local Visions into National Solutions," 2003.

[179] P.L. 111-296. For information, see CRS Report R41354, *Child Nutrition and WIC Reauthorization: P.L. 111-296.*

[180] P.L. 110-246, §4304.

[181] A "marker bill" is used to introduce specific measures or issues into a larger legislative debate. Such legislation is generally proposed as a "placeholder" for specific aspects of a larger bill, such as the farm bill, and allows legislators to include key provisions in the larger bill debate while it is still at the committee or subcommittee level.

[182] See, for example, Representative Earl Blumenauer's report, "Growing Opportunities: Family Farm Values for Reforming the Farm Bill."

[183] Hearing before the Senate Committee Agriculture on Agriculture, Nutrition, and Forestry, "Healthy Food Initiatives, Local Production, and Nutrition," March 7, 2012, http://www.ag.senate.gov/hearings/.

[184] See Senate briefing "Path to the 2012 Farm Bill: Senate Briefing on Local Food and Nutrition," March 2, 2012; House briefing "Investing in the Next Generation of Farmers," March 5, 2012; and House briefing "How Smart Food Systems Promote Economic Security for our Farmers and Food Security for All Americans," March 28, 2012.

---

changes to several USDA programs in the farm bill covering commodity support and crop insurance, farm credit, conservation, nutrition, rural development, research, and horticulture and livestock programs. The proposed changes would have expanded support for local and regional food production and farming systems. Other bills, including the Fresh Regional Eating for Schools and Health Act of 2011 (**S. 2016**; Wyden) and the Growing Opportunities for Agriculture and Responding to Markets Acts of 2011 and 2013 (**S. 1888** (112th Congress) and **S. 678** (113th Congress); Casey) also proposed to increase access to loans for small and beginning farmers, and other groups.[185]

The Community Agriculture Development and Jobs Act (**H.R. 3225**; Kaptur) also targeted enhanced support for non-traditional agricultural producers, and had been re-introduced from the 111th Congress. The bill identified specific changes to the farm bill and proposed to create a new USDA Office of Community Agriculture to ensure support for rural and non-rural food programs, provide grants and outreach for local food initiatives, promote consumption of fruits and vegetables, and eliminate food deserts. Another bill, the Healthy Food for Healthy Living Act (**H.R. 3291**; Velazquez) proposed providing grants to organizations operating in low-income communities to promote access to fresh fruits and vegetables and other foods. The Local Food for Healthy Families Act of 2013 (**H.R. 3072**; Kildee) would also provide grants for projects to provide incentives to low-income families receiving Supplemental Nutrition Assistance Program (SNAP) benefits (formerly food stamps) to purchase fruits and vegetables.

Other 112th Congress bills focused at the farm production level included the Beginning Farmer and Rancher Opportunity Act of 2011 (**H.R. 3236/S. 1850**; Walz/Harkin), which proposed to expand opportunities for beginning farmers and ranchers through changes to several USDA programs covering conservation; rural development; research, education, and extension; and farm credit and crop insurance. Separately, the Community-Supported Agriculture Promotion Act (**H.R. 4012/S. 1414**; Welch/Sanders) proposed to establish a community-supported agriculture promotion program, similar to USDA farmers' market program, to expand and develop CSAs, among other goals. The Veterans Gardens Employment and Opportunity Act (**H.R. 3905**; Baca) proposed to use gardens as a means to employ veterans.

Other bills actively addressed concerns about food deserts. The Healthy Food Financing Initiative (**H.R. 3525/S. 1926** (112th Congress) and **H.R. 2343/S. 821** (113th Congress); Schwartz/Gillibrand), re-introduced from the 111th Congress, proposed to increase investments in food financing to reduce the number of food deserts nationwide, as well as address childhood obesity. Representative Fudge also introduced two comprehensive bills—the Let's Grow Acts of 2011 and 2013 (**H.R. 4351** (112th Congress) and **H.R. 1933** (113th Congress)) and the Fit for Life Act of 2011 and 2014 (**H.R. 2795** (112th Congress) and **H.R. 4765** (113th Congress))—that proposed to improve the nutritional quality of and access to foods in underserved communities and to expand certain child nutrition programs and other domestic feeding programs.

Other bills focused on nutrition while proposing also to expand markets for local producers. The Local School Foods Act (**H.R. 3092**; Welch) proposed a pilot program to increase the amount of purchases of local fresh fruits and vegetables for schools and service institutions by giving certain states the option of receiving a USDA grant instead of receiving commodities under the agency's commodity procurement programs. The Eat Local Foods Act (**H.R. 1722**; Pingree) proposed a grant to states to provide schools with local food credits equal to a portion of the total value of the

---

[185] For more information, see CRS Report RS21977, *Agricultural Credit: Institutions and Issues*.

commodity assistance (or cash payments in lieu thereof). Two bills, **S. 1593** (Gillibrand) and **H.R. 1722** (Pingree), would have made it easier for farmers' markets, roadside stands, and other farm-to-consumer venues to participate as licensed retailers in SNAP.[186]

Considerations for Congress

Farm bill legislation enacted in both 2008 and 2014 included a few provisions that directly support local and regional food systems, as well as reauthorized several programs that benefit all U.S. agricultural producers, including local and regional food producers. Despite these gains, many community and farm advocacy groups continue to argue that such food systems should play a larger policy role within the farm bill, and that the laws should be revised to reflect broader, more equitable policies across a range of production systems, including local food systems.

Many in Congress have historically defended the existing farm support programs as a means to ensure that the United States has continued access to the "most abundant, safest, and most affordable food supplies in the world." However, there are long-standing criticisms of the traditional farm subsidy programs administered by USDA. Some criticize the fact that the core farm bill programs are focused on selected commodities—corn, wheat, cotton, rice, soybeans, dairy, and sugar—and there have been calls from both inside and outside Congress to revamp U.S. farm programs. Among other program criticisms are concerns about the overall effectiveness of farm programs and the cost to taxpayers and consumers, as well as questions about whether continued farm support is even necessary, given that many support programs were established many decades ago and are considered by some to be no longer compatible with current national economic objectives, global trading rules, and federal budgetary or regulatory policies.

In addition to calls for increased equity among all U.S. food producers—regardless of farm size, type of food, or how it is produced—various programmatic changes have been proposed, some of which dovetail with efforts by supporters of local food systems. For example, it may be argued that other proposals introduced in the 112th Congress to address existing restrictions on planting fruits, vegetables, and wild rice on program crop base acreage (**H.R. 2675/S. 1427**; Ribble/Lugar) also had a "local" component, in that if these restrictions were removed the ability to grow fruits and vegetables on base acres could potentially provide benefits to producers in some regions.[187]

Supporters of an increased role for local food systems within the farm bill cite the increasing popularity of local foods, given perceived higher product quality and freshness, and a general belief that purchasing local foods helps support local farm economies and/or farmers that use certain production practices that may be more environmentally sustainable. Rising popularity is attributed to both increasing consumer demand and a desire among agricultural producers to take advantage of market opportunities within local and regional markets. Others contend that subsidizing the more traditional agriculture producers creates a competitive disadvantage to other producers who do not receive such support.

---

[186] Under current law, states receive a 50% federal match for electronic benefit transfer machines which are provided to approved retailers. These bills seek to make these matching funds available for farm-to-consumer retailers who need a wireless machine – currently not eligible for government financing. H.R. 1722 includes a pilot project that would include the pursuit of mobile smartphone technology for this purpose.

[187] Comments from Doug Sombke, South Dakota Farmers Union, Institute of Medicine of the National Academies (OIM-NAS), "Farm and Food Policy: Relationship to Obesity Prevention," May 19, 2011.

However, some may be opposed to extending farm bill support to local and regional food systems, which traditionally have not been a major constituency among other long-standing U.S. agricultural interests. Those opposed to extending farm bill benefits to local food systems cite concerns about overall limited financial resources to support U.S. agricultural producers as well as concerns that the most efficient and productive use of natural resources be employed for producing food. As shown by challenges from some in Congress to USDA's "Know Your Farmer, Know Your Food" initiative, there are concerns about the perceived priorities of USDA and fear that a shift in priorities may result in fewer resources for "conventional farmers who produce the vast majority of our nation's food supply" (see discussion in ""Know Your Farmer, Know Your Food" Initiative"). Other criticisms highlight the lack of an established definition of what constitutes a "local food" and also perception that USDA's support of local foods is mostly targeted to affluent consumers in urban areas, rather than farmers in rural communities.

Table 2. Selected USDA Programs that Potentially Support Local and Regional Food Systems

USDA agency	Program Name / CFDA#	Program Type	Eligible Applicants	Assistance Amount	Total Funding Type/Amount
AMS	Specialty Crop Block Grant Program (SCBGP), 10.170.	Formula grants.	State departments of agriculture, in partnership with organizations.	Varies by state. Base grant (about $180,000 per state), plus additional funds based on the state's share of the total value and acreage of U.S. specialty crop production. In FY2013, grants ranged from $180,000 to $18 million. Also provides multistate project grants.	Mandatory, totaling $72.5 million annually (FY2014-2017) and $85 million for FY2018 and each year thereafter. Funding for multistate project grants shall rise from $1 million (FY2014) to $5 million (FY2018). Local share: Unknown.
AMS	Farmers' Market and Local Food Promotion Program, 10.168.	Project grants.	Farmer coops, associations, nonprofit/public benefit corporations, local authorities, regional farmers' markets.	Limited to $100,000, with a minimum award of $5,000. Individual grants have averaged about $50,000.	Mandatory, $30 million annually (FY2014-FY2018), plus authorized appropriations of $10 million each year. Local share: Unknown.
AMS	Federal State Marketing Improvement Program (FSMIP), 10.156.	Project grants.	State agriculture departments and experiment stations, other state agencies.	Grants have ranged from $21,000 to $135,000, averaging $51,385. Matching funds required.	Discretionary, about $1.3 million appropriated annually. Local share: Unknown.
RD	Value-Added Agricultural Product Market Development Grants, 10.352.	Project grants.	Individual farmers, agriculture producer groups, farmer and rancher cooperatives, and majority-controlled producer-based businesses, and veterans.	Maximum grant amounts: $100,000 (planning grant) and $300,000 (working capital grant). Grant funds may be used to pay up to 50% of a project's costs. Applicant must contribute at least 50% in cash or in-kind contributions.	Mandatory, $63 million, available until expended, plus authorized annual appropriations of $40 million (FY2012-2018). Local share: Unknown.
NIFA	Beginning Farmer and Rancher Development Program (BFRDP), 10.311.	Project grants.	State, tribal, local, or regionally based networks/partnerships of public and private entities. At least 5% funds for veterans.	Up to $250,000 per year for up to 3 years. Matching funds are required.	Mandatory, $20 million annual (FY2014-FY2018), plus authorized annual appropriations of $40 million through FY2018). Local share: Unknown.
FSA	Microloan Program	Loans	Beginning, niche, and smaller family farm operations	Up to $35,000. Repayment term may vary and may not exceed seven years.	Administered through FSA's Operating Loan Program (CFDA# 10.406).
NIFA	Small Business Innovation Research (SBIR), 10.212.	Project grants.	Small businesses (fewer than 500 employees).	Grant limited to $100,000 and $500,000, and on the type and phase of the project.	Discretionary; appropriated funding has ranged from $17 million to $19 million (FY2010-FY2012). Local share: Unknown.
RMA, NRCS, AMS	Agricultural Management Assistance (AMA), 10.917.	Direct payments for specified use.	Agricultural producers who voluntarily address certain farmland conservation issues.	Provides technical and financial assistance of up to 75% of the cost of installing certain practices. Total AMA payments shall not exceed $50,000 per participant per year.	Mandatory, $15 million annually (FY2008-FY2012), allocated to NRCS (50%), RMA (40%), and AMS (10%). Local share: Unknown.
RMA	Community Outreach and Assistance Partnership Program (COAPP), 10.455	Disseminate technical information; training	Educational institutions, state ag departments, community organizations, farmer/rancher associations, nonprofits.	Assistance is through a cooperative agreement, ranging from $20,000 to $100,000 per agreement. No matching funds are required.	In 2013, RMA awards totaled nearly $10 million through two RMA programs. Local share: Unknown.

USDA agency	Program Name / CFDA#	Program Type	Eligible Applicants	Assistance Amount	Total Funding Type/Amount
USDA, Office of Outreach and Advocacy	Outreach and Assistance to Socially Disadvantaged Farmers and Ranchers (OASDFR), 10.443.	Project grants.	Land grant institutions, state-controlled institutions, Indian tribes, veterans, Latino-serving institutions, nonprofits, community organizations.	Grants range from $100,000 to $400,000 per year for up to 3 years, with no matching requirements.	Mandatory/discretionary. Mandatory funds of $10 million per year (FY2014-FY2018), authorized appropriations of $20 million annually through FY2018. Local share: Unknown.
RD	Rural Cooperative Development Grant (RCDG), 10.771.	Project grants.	Nonprofit corporations including universities.	1-year grants up to $225,000, with matching requirements. Maximum award amount per Small Socially-Disadvantaged Producer Grant is $200,000.	Discretionary. Appropriations authorized $40 million annually (FY2014-FY2018).
RD	Business and Industry (B&I) Guaranteed Loans, 10.768.	Direct and guaranteed loans.	Individual, nonprofits, business,	Guaranteed loans up to $10 million, with special exceptions for loans up to $25 million. The Secretary may approve guaranteed loans up to $40 million, for rural cooperative organizations that process value-added agricultural commodities.	Obligations were $1.3 billion in FY2010, and $1.2 billion in FY2011. Local share: At least 5% by law.
RD	Community Facilities (CF), 10.766.	Direct and guaranteed loans; project grants.	Public and nonprofit organizations, and Indian tribes.	Direct loans range from $5,000 to $9 million (average: $828,407); guaranteed loans range from $26,000 to $20 million (average: $2.8 million); and project grants range from $300 to $0.4 million. No matching requirements.	Direct loans: $290 million (FY2011); guaranteed loans: $196 million (FY2011); project grants: $28 million (FY2011). Local share: Unknown.
RD	Rural Business Development Grants program (consolidating Rural Business Enterprise Grants & Rural Business Opportunity Grants)	Project grants.	Rural public entities (towns, communities, state agencies, and authorities) rural nonprofit corporations, rural Indian tribes, and cooperatives.	Details of new consolidated program subject to USDA rulemaking. Previously grants generally ranged from $10,000 up to $150,000, with no matching requirements.	Authorized appropriations of $65 million annually (FY2014-FY2018) to remain available until expended. Local share: Unknown.
RD	Rural Microentrepreneur Assistance Program (RMAP), 10-870.	Loans and technical assistance grants.	Microenterprise Development Organizations (MDOs), or other nonprofit, Indian tribe or public institution of higher education serving rural areas.	Loans range from a minimum of $50,000 to a maximum of $500,000 for a single loan in any given fiscal year. Grants are awarded up to $130,000, with matching requirements.	Mandatory: $3 million annually (FY2014-FY2018), plus authorized appropriations of $40 million annually (FY2014-FY2018). Local share: Unknown.
NIFA	Sustainable Agriculture Research and Education (SARE), 10.215.	Project grants.	Individual farmers/ranchers, extension agents and university educators, researchers, nonprofits, and communities.	Varies depending on the type of grant and the region, ranging from $1,000 for a producer grant or $350 for a research grant.	Discretionary. Appropriated funding averaging $13 million to $14 million annually (FY2010-FY2012). Local share: Unknown.
FNS	WIC Farmers' Market Nutrition Program (WIC-FMNP), 10.572.	Formula grants.	State health, agriculture and other agencies and Indian tribes.	Varies by state. In FY2013, grants ranged from $6,300 to $3.1 million.	Discretionary. $16.5 million appropriated in FY2014. Local share: Unknown.

USDA agency	Program Name / CFDA#	Program Type	Eligible Applicants	Assistance Amount	Total Funding Type/Amount
FNS	Senior Farmers' Market Nutrition Program (SFMNP), 10.576.	Project grants.	State health, agriculture and other agencies and Indian tribes.	Varies by state. In FY2013, grants ranged from $9,900 to $1.8 million.	Mandatory, $20.6 million annually through FY2018. Local share: Unknown.
FNS	Food Insecurity Nutrition Incentive	Project grants.	State health, agriculture and other agencies and Indian tribes.	TBD.	Mandatory, $100 million (FY2014-2018), plus discretionary authority of $5 million per year. Local share: Unknown.
FNS	Farm to School, 10.579.	Project grants.	Eligible schools, state and local agencies, Indian tribes, agricultural producers/groups, nonprofits organizations.	Maximum grant amount shall not exceed $100,000, and the federal share may not exceed 75% of the total project cost.	Mandatory funding set at $5 million starting on October 1, 2012, and each October 1 thereafter, plus appropriations "such sums as necessary" (FY2011-FY2015). Local share: Unknown.
FNS	School Gardens, 10.579.	Project grants.	The pilot shall target not more than five states (either a school-based or a community-based summer program).	USDA's People's Garden School Pilot Program was awarded to Washington State University and will serve students attending 70 elementary schools (WA, NY, IA, AR).	The 2008 farm bill did not authorize appropriations to carry out the provision, but USDA allocated $1 million to the Peoples' Garden School Pilot Program.
FNS	Provision within commodity procurement through "DoD Fresh" program.	Allows geographic preference regarding purchases.	Eligible schools, state and local agencies.	Provision is structured as a preference and does not require states and school food authorities to include geographic preference in their procurement.	The 2008 farm bill did not authorize appropriations or designate how much participating states should spend in carrying out this provision. 2014 farm bill also requires USDA to pilot up to 8 states using local sourcing instead of DoD Fresh.
(TBD)	Healthy Food Financing Initiative (as authorized in the 2014 farm bill)	Loans, grants, tech. state, or local public-private partnership.	Partnerships involving regional, assistance.	TBD.	The 2014 farm bill authorizes appropriations up to $125 million, to remain available until expended.
NIFA	Food and Agriculture Service Learning Program	Project grants.	Eligible entities that carry out statutory purposes.	TBD.	Appropriations up to $25 million to remain available until expended.
NIFA	Community Food Projects (CFP), 10.225.	Project grants.	Private non-profit entities.	Amount and duration vary depending on type of grant all require a match in resources. (Separate grant for a healthy urban food enterprise development center.)	Mandatory, $9 million in FY2015 and each year thereafter.

Source: Compiled by CRS. Funding levels shown are those available for all U.S. farming operations and food distribution systems, regardless of size and distance from market. Data are not available to determine share of available funding for the highlighted program used to support local and regional food systems. Programs are grouped according to their listing in the **Appendix**; groupings are not intended to indicate any rank or importance.

Notes: "Mandatory" means funding is available without an annual appropriation, and usually funded through the Commodity Credit Corporation (CCC). "Discretionary" requires an annual appropriation by Congress. Where the funding source could not be readily determined, available data on obligations/awards are provided. USDA agencies include Agricultural Marketing Service (AMS), Rural Development (RD), Risk Management Agency (RMA), National Institute of Food and Agriculture (NIFA), Farm Service Agency (FSA), Agricultural Research Service (ARS), Natural Resources Conservation Service (NRCS), and Food and Nutrition Service (FNS).

Appendix. Overview of Selected Federal Programs

Following is a listing of generally available federal farm support and grant programs that may provide support and assistance to local and regional food production systems. However, except as noted, these programs are not limited or targeted to local or regional food systems. These federal programs are grouped into the following broad program categories (grouped by type of support and not intended to indicate any rank or importance):

- marketing and promotion;

- business assistance;

- rural and community development;[188] and

- nutrition and education.

These programs are summarized in **Table 2** above. Many of the programs reviewed below are highlighted as part of the Administration's "Know Your Farmer, Know Your Food" initiative, among other USDA documentation.[189] Other programs have been identified by the National Sustainable Agriculture Coalition (NSAC) in its *Guide to USDA Funding for Local and Regional Food Systems*, as well as various state or regional initiatives that are listed in the appendix of NSAC's report.[190] A primary source of information on these selected programs is from the Catalog of Federal Domestic Assistance.[191]

This appendix does not provide a comprehensive listing of all possible USDA programs that might benefit local and regional food systems. Instead, it focuses on selected USDA grant and loan programs administered by the Agricultural Marketing Service (AMS), the Rural Development (RD) agencies, and the Food and Nutrition Service (FNS).

Although this appendix provides some information on a few programs administered by other USDA agencies, it does not review many of the broad-based conservation and research programs that provide benefits to a range of agricultural producers, including producers engaged in local and regional food production systems, either directly or indirectly.[192] These programs are

---

[188] For more information, see CRS Report RL31837, *An Overview of USDA Rural Development Programs*. USDA links to state or local office information is at http://www.rurdev.usda.gov/recd_map.html. For most programs, "rural areas" are defined as any area except a city or town where the population exceeds 50,000, or any urbanized area contiguous or adjacent to a town with more than 50,000 people (7 U.S.C. §1991(a)(13)(A)).

[189] USDA, "Grants, Loans, and Support," (http://www.usda.gov/wps/portal/usda/usdahome?navid=KYF_GRANTS); "Family and Small Farms" (http://www.nifa.usda.gov/familysmallfarms.cfm); and "USDA Resources for Local Food Systems" (http://www.csrees.usda.gov/nea/food/in_focus/health_if_usda_local_food html).

[190] Including partnerships and university programs located in Iowa, Illinois, Michigan, Minnesota, New York, North Carolina, Ohio, Oregon, Washington, Wisconsin, and other states. Also, presentations from Drake University Law School conference, "America's New Farmers: Policy Innovations and Opportunities," Washington DC, March 2010.

[191] CFDA has detailed program descriptions for more than 2,000 federal assistance programs (https://www.cfda.gov).

[192] For more information, see CRS Report R40763, *Agricultural Conservation: A Guide to Programs* and CRS Report R40819, *USDA's Research, Education, and Economics (REE) Mission Area: Issues and Background*. Information on how these programs contribute to local and regional food systems are outlined in memos from USDA Deputy Secretary Kathleen A. Merrigan "Harnessing USDA Natural Resources Conservation Service Programs to Support Local and Regional Food Systems," January 21, 2011, http://www.usda.gov/documents/nrcs-memo.pdf, and "USDA Research, Education, and Economics Support for Local and Regional Food Systems," October 27, 2009, http://www.usda.gov/documents/ KnowYourFarmerandREE.pdf.

---

authorized by the periodic omnibus farm bill. USDA's conservation programs are administered by the Natural Resources Conservation Service (NRCS) and the Farm Service Agency (FSA), and provide financial and technical assistance, as well as competitive grants, as part of a range of programs administered by these USDA agencies. USDA's research and extension programs are administered by the Agricultural Research Service (ARS) or the National Institute of Food and Agriculture (NIFA), and provide funding to states and local partners through various mechanisms, such as formula funds, competitive grants, and other programs.[193]

The funding levels reported for these selected programs are those available, in some cases, for all U.S. farming operations and food distribution systems, regardless of size and location from market. Data are not available to determine share of available funding for these programs used to support local and regional food systems, compared to all other types of farming systems. Only a few cases exist where there is a statutory requirement supporting local production, such as in the 5% set-aside of total Business and Industry (B&I) loans, or the option to make local purchases under USDA's Farm to School program. For many of these programs, most indications are that the share used to support local food systems is likely very small.

Marketing and Promotion

Specialty Crop Block Grant Program

The Specialty Crop Block Grant Program (SCBGP), administered by AMS, was authorized in the Specialty Crops Competitiveness Act of 2004 (P.L. 108-465), and further amended by the 2008 farm bill.[194] Under the program, USDA provides block grants to the state departments of agriculture within the 50 states, the District of Columbia, and the U.S. territories to enhance the competitiveness of specialty crops. The program is funded through USDA's Commodity Credit Corporation (CCC),[195] and is therefore mandatory, available without an annual (or discretionary) appropriation. Program funding will have totaled $375 million over the FY2014-FY2018 period: $72.5 million annually (FY2014-2017) and $85 million for FY2018 and each year thereafter. Funding for multistate project grants shall rise from $1 million (FY2014) to $5 million (FY2018) and be available until expended.

Under the program, each state receives a base grant plus additional funds based on the state's share of the total value of U.S. specialty crop production.[196] California, Florida, and Washington have been the three largest recipients under this program, accounting for nearly one-half of all available funds. How each state spends its allocation depends on its priorities. In FY2013, a total of 694 projects were funded covering marketing and promotion (26% of projects), education

---

[193] USDA's Current Research Information System (CRIS) is the agency's documentation and reporting system for ongoing and recently completed research and education projects. See http://cris.csrees.usda.gov/.

[194] P.L. 110-246, §10109; 7 U.S.C. §1621 note (CFDA# 10.170). "Specialty crop" is defined as: "fruits and vegetables, tree nuts, dried fruits, and horticulture and nursery crops (including floriculture)." See also "USDA Definition of Specialty Crop" (http://www.ams.usda.gov/AMSv1.0/getfile?dDocName=STELPRDC5082113).

[195] USDA's Commodity Credit Corporation is a government-owned corporation that is authorized to borrow up to $30 billion at any one time from the U.S. Treasury. The CCC mainly is a financing mechanism for farm bill programs such as commodity price and income supports, agricultural conservation, export assistance, and other authorizations.

[196] The minimum base grant each state is eligible to receive is equal to the higher of $100,000 or 1/3 of 1% of the total amount of funding made available for that year. The base grant portion is about $180,000 per state. The additional allocation is based on the value and acreage of specialty crop production in each state relative to national production.

(23%), research (15%), pest and plant health (16%), food safety (8%), and production (6%), among other types of projects (6%).[197] USDA's annual report describes the funded projects across all states.[198] Among the types of projects funded by the program are school and community gardens; farm-to-school programs; certification and training for farmers; facilities that support the processing, aggregation, and distribution of locally grown specialty crops; and improved access to specialty crops in underserved communities.[199] A report by the National Farm to School Network indicates that many states have funded farm-to-school programs using these program funds.[200]

Farmers' Market and Local Food Promotion Program

USDA's farmers' market and various other direct-to-consumer marketing programs provide for market access and assistance to small and medium-size farmers, including fruit and vegetable growers. The intent of the Farmer-to-Consumer Direct Marketing Act of 1976 (P.L. 94-463) was to promote the "development and expansion of direct marketing of agricultural commodities from farmers to consumers" through a range of marketing channels including farmers' markets, farm stands, and roadside stands, community-supported agriculture (CSA), "pick-your-own" farms, Internet marketing, and other types of niche markets. The act originally authorized the Farmers' Market Promotion Program (FMPP), administered by AMS, which was amended in subsequent farm bills.[201] The 2014 farm bill reauthorized and expanded the program to include local and regional food enterprises that process, distribute, aggregate, store, and market locally or regionally produced food products, also renaming it the Farmers' Market and Local Food Promotion Program. Under the reauthorized program, two competitive grant programs are available: FMPP and the Local Food Promotion Program (LFPP).

The 2014 farm bill increased mandatory funding from previous funding levels of about $10 million annually to $30 million annually (FY2014-FY2018), and separately authorized appropriations of $10 million each year. Each program is designated 50% of available funding.

Other USDA-administered farmer's markets programs geared more toward nutrition assistance are highlighted in the section of the report titled "Farmers' Market Nutrition Programs" and also "Supplemental Nutrition Assistance Program (SNAP) at Farmers' Markets."

Farmers' Market Promotion Program (FMPP)

FMPP provides $15 million in annual mandatory funding available for marketing support for farmers markets and other direct to consumer outlets.[202] Under FMPP, USDA provides grants to establish, improve, and promote farmers' markets and other direct marketing activities such as roadside stands, community supported agriculture (CSAs), pick-your-own farms, agritourism, direct sales to schools, and other direct marketing activities. Activities may include promotion,

---

[197] AMS, "Funded Projects," http://www.ams.usda.gov/AMSv1.0/getfile?dDocName=STELPRDC5093992.

[198] Ibid. USDA's report provides a full listing of all program recipients by state, applicant name, and grant amount.

[199] USDA, "Grants, Loans, and Support," http://www.usda.gov/wps/portal/usda/usdahome?navid=KYF_GRANTS.

[200] Farm to School Network, "Specialty Crop Block Grant Program Funded Projects Project SubType - Farm to School," http://www.farmtoschool.org/files/publications_267.pdf. The summary covers the FY2006-2009 period.

[201] P.L. 94-463, as amended; 7 U.S.C. § 3005 (CFDA# 10.168).

[202] AMS, http://www.ams.usda.gov/AMSv1.0/fmpp.

---

outreach, and advertising; education for farmers and growers in marketing and business planning; and infrastructure purchases, such as refrigerated trucks, or equipment for a commercial kitchen for value-added products.[203] Grants are also available to bring local farm products into federal nutrition programs through electronic benefits transfer (EBT) technology at direct-market outlets in order to accept Supplemental Nutrition Assistance Program (SNAP, formerly the food stamp program) benefits. In addition to SNAP, FNS administers two other related programs: the WIC Farmers' Market Nutrition Program (WIC-FMNP)[204] and the Senior Farmers' Market Nutrition Program (SFMNP).[205] These two programs allow for farmers' market purchases by low-income WIC applicants and recipients and also low-income seniors, usually through the use of redeemable coupons.

Eligible entities include farmer cooperatives, grower associations, nonprofit/public benefit corporations, local governments, economic development corporations, and regional farmers' market authorities, among others. Grant awards are limited to $100,000, with a minimum award of $15,000. Matching funds are not required. A listing of previous awards is at USDA's website.

Local Food Promotion Program (LFPP)

LFPP provides $15 million in annual mandatory funding available for marketing and promotional support specifically for local food businesses, including food hubs, delivery and aggregation businesses, and processing and storage facilities along the local food supply chain. Two types of project applications are accepted under LFPP: planning grants and implementation grants. Applicants can apply for either project but will receive only one type of grant per grant cycle.

- LFPP Planning Grants for planning stages of establishing or expanding a local and regional food business enterprise. Activities may include market research, feasibility studies, and business planning. A minimum of $5,000 and a maximum of $25,000 may be awarded per proposal, and the grants must be completed within a 12 month period; extension will not exceed an additional 6 months.

- LFPP Implementation Grants for establishing a new local and regional food business enterprise, or to improve or expand an existing local or regional food business enterprise. Activities may include training and technical assistance for the business enterprise and/or for producers working with the business enterprise; outreach and marketing to buyers and consumers; working capital; and non-construction infrastructure improvements to business enterprise facilities or information technology systems. A minimum of $25,000 and a maximum of $100,000 will be awarded per proposal, and the grants must be completed within a 24 month grant period; extension will not exceed an additional 6 months.

Eligible entities include entities that "support local and regional food business enterprises that process, distribute, aggregate, or store locally or regionally produced food products."[206] Such entities may include agricultural businesses, agricultural cooperatives, producer networks, producer associations, community supported agriculture networks, community supported

---

[203] USDA, "Grants, Loans, and Support," http://www.usda.gov/wps/portal/usda/usdahome?navid=KYF_GRANTS.

[204] FNS, "Grant Levels by State, FY 2006-2011," http://www.fns.usda.gov/wic/FMNP/FMNPgrantlevels.htm.

[205] FNS, "SFMNP Grant Levels, FY 2006-2011," http://www.fns.usda.gov/wic/SeniorFMNP/SFMNPgrantlevels.htm.

[206] AMS, http://www.ams.usda.gov/AMSv1.0/lfpp.

agriculture associations, and other agricultural business entities (for-profit groups); nonprofit corporations; public benefit corporations; economic development corporations; regional farmers' market authorities; and local and tribal governments. Grant funds require a 25% match.

Federal State Marketing Improvement Program

The Federal State Marketing Improvement Program (FSMIP) was authorized in the Agricultural Marketing Act of 1946.[207] Administered by AMS, the program provides matching funds to state departments of agriculture, state agricultural experiment stations, and other appropriate state agencies to provide new market opportunities for U.S. food and agricultural products and to encourage research and innovation to improve the efficiency and performance of the marketing system. Matching funds are required. In addition to the projects that are geared toward developing and improving production and marketing of agricultural products, FSMIP specifically encourages state agencies to submit proposals to enhance rural communities by developing local and regional food systems and value-added agriculture, as well as direct marketing opportunities for producers, or producer groups. Eligible projects may include determining market demand for local products; building online marketing tools such MarketMaker; developing protocols for harvesting excess crops for local food banks; and developing business plans for food hubs.[208] A list of previously funded projects is at USDA's website.[209] In recent years, FSMIP grants have ranged from $21,000 to $135,000 each. USDA has received about $1.3 million annually in appropriated funding for the program, which has been used to fund 20-25 projects, averaging about $50,000 each.

Business Assistance

Value-Added Agricultural Product Market Development Grants

The Value-Added Agricultural Product Market Development Grants was originally authorized as the Value-Added Producer Grants (VAPG) program in the Agricultural Risk Act of 2000, and amended by subsequent farm bills.[210] The 2014 farm bill (P.L. 113-79, § 6203) renamed the program and expanded its scope and available funding.

The program, administered by USDA's Rural Business-Cooperative Service, provides grants to eligible entities, such as independent agricultural commodity producers, agricultural producer groups, farmer and rancher cooperatives, and majority-controlled producer-based businesses, to develop strategies and business plans to further refine, enhance, or otherwise add value to their products. Grants may be used for planning activities (such as development of feasibility studies, business plans, and marketing strategies) and for working capital to implement a marketing strategy for value-added agricultural products and for farm-based renewable energy. The maximum grant amount of a planning grant is $100,000 and of a working capital grant is $300,000. Grant funds may be used to pay up to 50% of a project's costs, with the applicant

---

[207] 7 U.S.C. §1621-1627 (CFDA# 10.156). See USDA, AMS, "FY2011 FSMIP Guidelines", http://www.ams.usda.gov/AMSv1.0/FSMIP.

[208] USDA, "Grants, Loans, and Support," http://www.usda.gov/wps/portal/usda/usdahome?navid=KYF_GRANTS. Also see AMS, "FY2011 FSMIP Guidelines," http://www.ams.usda.gov/AMSv1.0/FSMIP.

[209] USDA AMS, "FSMIP Projects: 1990-Present," http://www.ams.usda.gov/AMSv1.0/FSMIP.

[210] P.L. 106-224, §6202; 7 U.S.C. §1621 note (CFDA# 10.352).

contributing at least 50% in cash or in-kind contributions.[211] Value-added producer grants offer another potential resource for local and regional food production systems to engage in market and product development, as well as to finance various value-added activities, such as further processing and packaging of raw agricultural commodities. In addition, the program provides priority funding for projects that contribute to opportunities for beginning farmers or ranchers, socially disadvantaged farmers or ranchers, and operators of small- and medium-sized family farms and ranches. The 2014 farm bill expanded eligibility to include to veteran farmers and ranchers veteran farmers or ranchers.

Available funding is both mandatory and subject to annual appropriations. The 2014 farm bill provided mandatory funding levels of $63 million, which is available until expended. Discretionary funding is authorized at $40 million annually from FY2012 to FY2018. Since the program began in 2001 the total amount of grant funding provided has ranged from about $15 million to more than $20 million annually. A full listing of previous program recipients by state, applicant name, and grant amount is available at USDA's website.

Beginning Farmer and Rancher Development Program

The Beginning Farmer and Rancher Development Program (BFRDP), administered by NIFA, was authorized in the 2002 farm bill.[212] The program provides competitive grants to new and established local and regional training, education, outreach, and technical assistance initiatives that address the needs of beginning farmers and ranchers. Grants are awarded to state, tribal, local, or regional networks or partnerships of public and private entities. Eligible project areas include production and land management strategies that enhance land stewardship; business management and decision support strategies that improve financial viability; marketing strategies for increased competitiveness; and legal strategies that assist with farm or land acquisition and transfer. The maximum amount of a grant is $250,000 per year and is limited to three years, with a 25% match in resources.

The program provides three types of grants, including (1) standard grants, which directly serve beginning farmers and ranchers, each up to $250,000 per year for a maximum of three years; (2) educational enhancements grants, which develop resources and provide coordination and support to standard grants for a particular topic or region;[213] and (3) clearinghouse grant, which provides one grant for a national site to house curricula, training materials, and other information for new farmers and ranchers and organizations that work with them. The 2014 farm bill (P.L. 113-79, § 7409) expanded available mandatory funding to $20 million per year (FY2014-FY2018), to be available until expended, and extends authority to appropriate $30 million annually through FY2018. Not less than 5% of available funds are to be used to support beginning farmers who are military veterans.

---

[211] USDA's website, http://www.rurdev.usda.gov/BCP_VAPG.html.

[212] P.L. 107-171, §7405; 7 U.S.C. §3319f (CFDA# 10.311). See USDA, ""Plan for Beginning Farmer and Rancher Development Program," March 6, 2014; and USDA's website: http://www.nifa.usda.gov/funding/bfrdp/bfrdp html.

[213] Previous topics have included environmental stewardship, financial management, farm safety, "farm beginnings" curriculum, individual development accounts.

USDA Microloan Program

In January 2013, USDA created a new microloan program within the existing direct farm operating loan program, using its regulatory prerogative, to "better serve the unique financial operating needs of beginning, niche and the smallest of family farm operations."[214] The program is administered through FSA's Operating Loan Program.[215]

FSA had found that small farm operations—including nontraditional farms, specialty crop producers, and operators of community-supported agriculture—had unique needs and limited financing options. FSA found these farms could face unintended barriers when applying for USDA operating loans, often because of experience requirements and pledging collateral. The microloan program simplifies and expedites the application process, and adds flexibility for meeting loan eligibility and security requirements. Microloans can be used for all approved operating expenses as authorized by the FSA Operating Loan Program, including initial start-up expenses; annual expenses (seed, fertilizer, utilities, land rents); marketing and distribution expenses; family living expenses; purchase of livestock, equipment, and other materials essential to farm operations; minor farm improvements such as wells and coolers; hoop houses to extend the growing season; essential tools; irrigation; and delivery vehicles. The maximum microloan size is $35,000. As of March 2014, USDA has issued more than 4,900 microloans totaling $97 million.[216]

The 2014 farm bill (P.L. 113-79, § 5106) authorized a similar program to allow USDA to contract with community-based, state entities or other intermediaries to make or guarantee loans or to provide related services.

Small Business Innovation Research

The Small Business Innovation Research (SBIR) program originated as part of the Small Business Innovation Development Act of 1982, as amended.[217] The program, administered by NIFA, provides grants to qualified small businesses to stimulate technological innovations in the private sector; strengthen the role of small businesses in meeting federal research and development needs; increase private sector commercialization of innovations derived from USDA-supported research and development efforts; and foster and encourage participation by women-owned and socially and economically disadvantaged small business firms in technological innovations. Eligible applicants include small businesses with fewer than 500 employees. Grant amounts are limited to $100,000 and $500,000 per project, and limited to eight months and to two years, respectively, depending on the type and phase of the project. Previously, grants have been awarded to small and mid-size farms and ranches that sells to local markets and to implement a CSA model to bring their locally grown food to inner city households and schools, among other types of projects.[218] A summary of funded projects is at USDA's website.[219] In

---

[214] FSA, "Microloan Fact Sheet," January 2013, http://fsa.usda.gov/Internet/FSA_File/microloans_eng_jan2013.pdf. Also see 78 *Federal Register* 12, 3828-3836, January 17, 2013. A proposed rule was issued in May 2012. For other information see CRS Report RS21977, *Agricultural Credit: Institutions and Issues.*

[215] Farm and Rural Development Act, as amended, P.L. 92-419, 7 U.S.C. 1942 (CFDA# 10.406).

[216] USDA, "Microloan Gets Getting Growing," March 25, 2014.

[217] P.L. 97-219; 15 U.S.C. §638 (CFDA# 10.212). Also: http://www.nifa.usda.gov/funding/sbir/sbir_synopsis.html.

[218] USDA, "SBIR," http://www.usda.gov/wps/portal/usda/usdahome?contentid=kyf_grants_nifa5_content.html.

[219] NIFA, "Abstracts of Funded SBIR Projects," http://www.nifa.usda.gov/funding/sbir/sbir_abstracts.html.

previous years, appropriated program funding has ranged from about $17 million to $19 million (FY2010-FY2012).

Agricultural Management Assistance

The Agricultural Management Assistance (AMA) program was authorized in the Agricultural Risk Protection Act of 2000,[220] and amended by subsequent farm bills. AMA is managed by three USDA agencies—NRCS, AMS, and the Risk Management Agency (RMA). The program provides assistance for producers in states traditionally underserved by federal crop insurance[221] to mitigate financial risk through production or marketing diversification or resource conservation practices. AMA is funded through the CCC at $15 million annually from FY2008 to FY2014, and the funding is allocated in statute as follows: NRCS (50%), RMA (40%), and AMS (10%).[222] The NRCS portion provides financial and technical assistance to farmers to voluntarily address issues such as water management, water quality, and erosion control by incorporating conservation into their farming operations.[223] The program provides technical and financial assistance of up to 75% of the cost of installing certain conservation practices. The RMA portion provides assistance to farmers to mitigate financial risk through production or marketing diversification, including support for direct marketing and value-added processing, and the development of new risk management approaches. RMA historically used AMA to provide assistance to producers for the purchase of Adjusted Gross Revenue (AGR) insurance but has recently been used to increase participation for buy-up insurance coverage.[224] The AMS portion provides support for transition to organic farming through organic certification cost share assistance. Total AMA payments from all three agencies cannot exceed $50,000 per participant for any fiscal year.

Community Outreach and Assistance Partnership Program

The Community Outreach and Assistance Partnership Program (COAPP), administered by RMA, is intended to ensure that women, limited resource, socially disadvantaged and other traditionally underserved producers of priority commodities are provided information and training necessary to use financial management, crop insurance, marketing contracts, and other existing and emerging risk management tools.[225] The program provides education, community outreach, and assistance in 47 states to help small and underserved producers get crop insurance education to effectively manage their risk and remain productive. Eligible applicants include educational institutions, community based organizations, associations of farmers and ranchers, state departments of agriculture, and other non-profit organizations. Assistance is through a cooperative agreement, ranging from $20,000 to $100,000 per agreement. No matching funds are required. In 2013, RMA awarded cooperative agreements totaling nearly $10 million from two

---

[220] P.L. 106-224, §524b; 7 U.S.C. §1524 (CFDA# 10.917).

[221] States include Connecticut, Delaware, Hawaii, Maryland, Massachusetts, Maine, Nevada, New Hampshire, New Jersey, New York, Pennsylvania, Rhode Island, Utah, Vermont, West Virginia, and Wyoming.

[222] P.L. 110-246, §2801.

[223] USDA, http://www.nrcs.usda.gov/wps/portal/nrcs/main/national/programs/financial/ama.

[224] The AGR provides a guaranteed revenue level for the whole farm and rewards more diversified farmers with higher coverage levels and smaller insurance premiums. Buy-up insurance provides higher coverage on crops and lower deductibles (referred to as the Financial Assistance Program); http://www.rma.usda.gov/bulletins/managers/2011/mgr-11-008.pdf. For more information, see CRS Report R40532, *Federal Crop Insurance: Background* .

[225] Federal Crop Insurance Act (P.L. 96-365), as amended; 7 U.S.C. §1522(d) (CFDA# 10.455). USDA, http://www.rma.usda.gov/aboutrma/civilrights/outreach html.

RMA programs, the Targeted States Program and the Risk Management Education Partnership Program.[226]

Outreach and Assistance to Socially Disadvantaged Farmers and Ranchers

The Outreach and Assistance to Socially Disadvantaged Farmers and Ranchers (OASDFR) program was first authorized in the 1990 farm bill, as amended.[227] Also referred to as the "Section 2501 program," it requires USDA to provide outreach and technical assistance to socially disadvantaged producers, defined as members of a group that has been subjected to racial or ethnic prejudice. The program provides competitive grants to land grant institutions (1862, 1890, or 1994), tribal governments and organizations, Latino-serving institutions, veterans, state-controlled institutions, and community-based organizations and nonprofits to provide outreach, training, education, financial assistance, and technical assistance, in order to encourage and assist socially disadvantaged farmers, ranchers, and forest landowners in owning and operating farms, ranches and non-industrial forest lands. OASDFR supports a range of outreach and assistance activities, including farm and financial management, marketing, and application and bidding procedures. Grants range from $100,000 to $400,000 per year for up to three years, and there are no matching requirements. The program is administered by USDA's new Office of Outreach and Advocacy.

Section 2501 was authorized at $25 million a year in the 2002 farm bill; however, the program has not received a congressional appropriation of more than $6 million in any year since. The 2014 farm bill (P.L. 113-79, § 12001) expanded funding for the program to provide $10 million per year in mandatory funding (FY2014-FY2018), plus authorized appropriations of $20 million annually through FY2018.

Rural and Community Development Programs

Rural Cooperative Development Grant

The Rural Cooperative Development Grant (RCDG) program was originally authorized in the 1990 farm bill, amending the Consolidated Farm and Rural Development Act (ConAct);[228] it was further amended in the 1996 and 2002 farm bills, and extended in subsequent farm bills. Administered by RD, the program provides project grants to nonprofit institutions, including universities, to establish and operate new or existing centers for rural cooperative development, value-added processing, and rural businesses, especially cooperatives.[229] Some eligible uses of funds include providing technical assistance, training and educating existing cooperatives; conducting feasibility studies and providing organizational guidance to new cooperatives; and

---

[226] "USDA Invests to Help Small and Underserved Producers Manage Risk and Remain Productive," October 2013.

[227] P.L. 101-624, §2501; 7 U.S.C. 2279 (CFDA# 10.443), as amended in the 2008 farm bill (P.L. 110-246, §14004). USDA, http://www.outreach.usda.gov/sdfr/index htm. See also CRS Report RS20430, *The Pigford Cases: USDA Settlement of Discrimination Suits by Black Farmers*.

[228] P.L. 101-624, §2347; ConAct §310B(e), 7 U.S.C. §1932 (CFDA# 10.771), P.L. 110-246, §6013. Formerly known as the Rural Technology and Cooperative Development Grant Program (RTCDG). USDA, http://www.rurdev.usda.gov/BCP_RCDG html.

[229] Cooperative development centers must primarily serve "rural areas" defined as any area except a city or town where the population exceeds 50,000, or any urbanized area contiguous or adjacent to a town with more than 50,000 people.

---

assessing the need and evaluating the potential support base for newly developing cooperatives.[230] The RCDG program has been used to support local food systems by establishing linkages with local food hubs, through the development and distribution of best practices and through training and technical assistance to farmer coperatives or any enterprises where multiple farmers collaborate thus providing for "scaling up" opportunities.[231]

Matching fund requirement are 25% of the total project cost for most eligible entities, but vary in some cases. Funding is discretionary, with authorized appropriations of $40 million annually (FY2014-FY2018); however, actual appropriated amounts have been lower than authorized levels. For FY2010, total funding for grants was $7.9 million, covering about 35 awards up to $225,000 each for a period of one year. FY2011 funds were an estimated $7.4 million.

Under the RCDG program, funds may be used for applications that focus on assistance to small, minority producers through their cooperative businesses. The Small Socially-Disadvantaged Producer Grant (SSDPG) is administered under the RCDG program.[232] SSDPG provides technical assistance to small, socially disadvantaged agricultural producers through eligible cooperatives and associations of cooperatives. Total program funding is estimated at about $3.5 million. The maximum award amount per grant is $200,000. No matching funds are required.

Business and Industry Guaranteed Loan Program

The Business and Industry (B&I) Guaranteed Loan Program was authorized as part of the ConAct, as amended in the 1996 and 2002 farm bills.[233] Administered by RD, the program provides guaranteed loans to help new and existing businesses in rural areas gain access to affordable capital. By issuing a guarantee to a private lender, USDA essentially co-signs the loan to a business owner, promising to pay a portion of any loss that might result if the business owner is unable to repay the loan. Having the guarantee reduces the lender's risk, allowing more favorable interest rates and terms. An eligible borrower may be an individual, a cooperative organization, corporation, partnership, or other legal entity (both for profit or nonprofit), or a federally recognized tribal group. Loans may be used to cover business and industrial acquisitions to prevent the business from closing; prevent the loss of employment opportunities, or provide expanded job opportunities; provide for business conversion, enlargement, repair, modernization, or development; purchase and develop land, easements, rights-of-way, buildings, or facilities; and purchase equipment, leasehold improvements, machinery, supplies, or inventory.

Guaranteed loans go up to $10 million with some special exceptions for loans up to $25 million. USDA may approve guaranteed loans up to $40 million for rural cooperative organizations that process value-added agricultural commodities. The maximum repayment for loans on real estate are not to exceed 30 years; machinery and equipment repayment are not to exceed the useful life of the machinery and equipment purchased with loan funds or 15 years, whichever is less; and working capital repayment are not to exceed 7 years. Program obligations were $1.3 billion in

---

[230] USDA, http://www.rurdev.usda.gov/BCP_RCDG html.

[231] USDA, "Grants, Loans, and Support," http://www.usda.gov/wps/portal/usda/usdahome?navid=KYF_GRANTS. Also, CRS communication with University of Illinois staff, September 15, 2011.

[232] USDA, http://www.rurdev.usda.gov/BCP_SSDPG html. Formerly the Small, Minority Producer Grant Program.

[233] 7 U.S.C §1932(g). §310B of the ConAct, as amended by P.L. 104-127 (§747) and P.L. 107-171 (§6017) (CFDA# 10.768). USDA, http://www.rurdev.usda.gov/rbs/busp/b&i_gar htm.

FY2010, and $1.2 billion in FY2011. Funds are allocated to states based on the proportion of their rural population, and funding for any local food initiatives would occur at the state level.

The 2008 farm bill further amended the B&I program to provide that at least 5% of available B&I program funding from FY2008 to FY2012 be used to support local and regional food production. This allocation of available funding is to be used to:

> make or guarantee loans to individuals, cooperatives, cooperative organizations, businesses, and other entities to establish and facilitate enterprises that process, distribute, aggregate, store, and market *locally or regionally produced agricultural food products* to support community development and farm and ranch income. [emphasis added]

An eligible "locally or regionally produced agricultural food product" is "any agricultural food product that is raised, produced, and distributed in ... the locality or region in which the final product is marketed, so that the total distance that the product is transported is less than 400 miles from the origin of the product; or ... the State in which the product is produced."[234] For FY2011, nearly $50 million was made available for local and regional food enterprises, with an estimated $41 million for FY2012.[235] An example of a local enterprise using B&I funds is Prairieland Foods in Nebraska, which received a $650,000 loan to purchase a new dairy processing facility to produce dairy products using locally sourced milk.[236]

Community Facilities

Community Facilities (CF) loans and grants were authorized in the Consolidated Farm and Rural Development Act, as amended.[237] Administered by RD, the program provides direct loans, guaranteed/insured loans, and project grants for the construction, acquisition, or renovation of community facilities or for the purchase of equipment for community facilities for public use in rural areas. Examples include, but are not limited to water and environmental projects, including water systems, waste systems, solid waste, and storm drainage facilities, as well as hospitals, fire protection, safety, and other community-based initiatives. Matching funds are not required. The size of the award varies by project, applicant's financial feasibility, and community size. Direct loans range from $5,000 to $9 million (average: $828,407); guaranteed loans range from $26,000 to $20 million (average: $2.8 million); and project grants range from $300 to $0.4 million (average $37,266). Eligible applicants include public and nonprofit organizations, and federally recognized Indian tribes. The proposed community facilities must be in rural areas, defined as areas with no more than 20,000 residents. In recent years, total funding for direct loans was $681 million (FY2010) and $290 million (FY2011). Funding for guaranteed loans was $292 million (FY2010) and $196 million (FY2011). Funding for project grants was $61 million (FY2010) and $28 million (FY2011).

An example of a project financed under the program is a $100,000 grant that was awarded to a medical center within an island community in Alaska to purchase two greenhouses for a community garden. Other types of local and regional projects that may qualify for CF funding include farmers' markets (e.g., structures); school and community kitchens; food banks, including

---

[234] P.L. 110-246, §6015.

[235] NSAC, "Local and Regional Food Enterprise Guaranteed Loans."

[236] USDA, "Grants, Loans, and Support," http://www.usda.gov/wps/portal/usda/usdahome?navid=KYF_GRANTS.

[237] P.L. 92-419, §306; 7 U.S.C. §1926 (CFDA#10.766). USDA, http://www rurdev.usda.gov/HCF_CF html.

refrigerators; community gardens (e.g., purchase land; water source access) and noncommercial greenhouses; and refrigerated trucks.[238]

Rural Business Development Grants

The 2014 farm bill (P.L. 113-79, § 6012) consolidated two previous USDA grant programs: the Rural Business Enterprise Grants (RBEG)[239] and the Rural Business Opportunity Grants (RBOG)[240] programs, renaming the new program Rural Business Development Grants program. Both programs were authorized under the ConAct, as amended, and reauthorized in the 2008 farm bill and administered by USDA's Rural Business-Cooperative Service. Both provided competitive grants to finance and facilitate a broad range of rural projects and promote sustainable economic development in rural communities. Eligible entities include rural public bodies, rural nonprofit corporations, rural Indian tribes, and cooperatives. The 2014 farm bill authorized appropriations of $65 million annually (FY2014-FY2018) to remain available until expended.

Details of new consolidated program will likely be subject to USDA rulemaking. Previously grants generally ranged from $10,000 up to $150,000, with no matching requirements. Examples of past funding under the two previous programs are as follows. RBEG provided funding for the development of small and emerging rural businesses, and employment-related adult education programs, and also provided funding to acquire and develop land and construct buildings, plants, equipment, access, parking areas, and utility and service extensions, among other activities. An specific example of RBEG funds supporting local food systems include a project grant to develop a mobile livestock unit in New York to provide local ranchers access to slaughter and processing equipment and local markets.[241] RBOG funding has covered regional economic planning focused on food system development; market development and feasibility studies; business training, including leadership development and technical assistance for entrepreneurs; and establishing business incubators, including commercial kitchens.[242] An example of RBOG funds supporting local food systems include a project grant to create FoodHub, an online marketplace based in Oregon that allows large-scale purchasers of food to connect with nearby growers.[243]

Rural Microentrepreneur Assistance Program

The Rural Microentrepreneur Assistance Program (RMAP) was authorized in the 2008 farm bill.[244] Administered by RD, the program provides direct loans and project grants to a Microenterprise Development Organizations (MDO), which may be a nonprofit organization, Indian tribe, or public institution of higher education that serves rural areas. An MDO may borrow $50,000 to $500,000 for a single loan in any given fiscal year. Loans can be used to provide working capital, equipment purchases, debt refinancing, business acquisitions, and

---

[238] USDA, "Grants, Loans, and Support," http://www.usda.gov/wps/portal/usda/usdahome?navid=KYF_GRANTS.

[239] 7 U.S.C. §1932(c)(2). §306 of the ConAct, as amended (CFDA#10.769).

[240] P.L. 104-127, §741, amending §306 of the ConAct, as amended; 7 U.S.C. §1926(a)(19)(C)(ii) (CFDA#10.773).

[241] USDA, "Grants, Loans, and Support," http://www.usda.gov/wps/portal/usda/usdahome?navid=KYF_GRANTS.

[242] A kitchen incubator refers to a business that provides for early-stage catering, retail and wholesale food businesses to a new small business where it can produce a food product. See databases at culinaryIncubator.com.

[243] USDA, "Grants, Loans, and Support," http://www.usda.gov/wps/portal/usda/usdahome?navid=KYF_GRANTS.

[244] P.L. 110-246, §6022, amending §306 of the ConAct; 7 U.S.C. §1926(a)(19)(C)(ii) (CFDA#10.870). USDA, http://www.rurdev.usda.gov/BCP_rmap html.

purchase or lease of real estate that is already improved (construction of any type is strictly prohibited). Grants are awarded up to $130,000, with matching requirements. Technical assistance grants can be used to provide training, education, operational support, business planning, market development assistance, and other related services to rural microentrepreneurs. Funding can cover financing a facility or equipment, business planning, and marketing, including coordinating and training necessary for a food hub or commercial kitchen incubator.[245] Mandatory funding through the CCC, which remains available until expended, is $3 million annually (FY2014-FY2018). In addition, appropriations are authorized at $40 million annually (FY2014-FY2018). However, in recent years no funds have been appropriated and the program received mandatory funding for some years only.

Research and Cooperative Extension

Sustainable Agriculture Research and Education

Sustainable Agriculture Research and Education (SARE), managed by NIFA, originated in the research provisions in the 1985 farm bill, aimed at enhancing low-input farming systems, and was expanded and renamed in the 1990 farm bill.[246] SARE provides a range of research and education grants in the areas of renewable energy, pest and weed management, pastured livestock and rotational grazing, no-till and conservation tillage, nutrient management, agroforestry, marketing, sustainable communities, systems research, and crop and livestock diversity, among other areas. Since 1988, SARE has funded nearly 5,000 projects with grants for farmers, ranchers, extension agents and university educators, researchers, nonprofits, students, and communities. Research and education grants, generally ranging from $60,000 to $150,000, fund projects that usually are interdisciplinary and involve scientists, producers, and others. Professional development grants, generally ranging from $20,000 to $90,000, offer educational opportunities for extension and NRCS, and for other agricultural professionals. Producer grants, typically between $1,000 and $15,000, go to farmers and ranchers who "test innovative ideas and share the results with their neighbors."[247] No individual organization matching funds are required. Program funds also support the dissemination of information on sustainable agriculture through clearinghouses such as the Alternative Farming Systems Information Center at USDA's National Agricultural Library, and the Sustainable Agriculture Network.

The program originated with a $3.9 million appropriation in FY1988. In recent years, funding for project grants has totaled $14.5 million (FY2010); and $13.5 million (FY2011 and also FY2012). State-by-state summaries and profiles of the SARE grants portfolio are available at SARE's website.[248]

---

[245] USDA, "Grants, Loans, and Support," http://www.usda.gov/wps/portal/usda/usdahome?navid=KYF_GRANTS.

[246] P.L. 101-624, §§1619-1624; 7 U.S.C. §5801 and 7 U.S.C §5812 (CFDA# 10.215). Originally part of P.L. 99-198, Subtitle C (Agricultural Productivity Research). Often referred to as "Low-Input Sustainable Agriculture" (LISA).

[247] USDA, http://www.nifa.usda.gov/fo/fundview.cfm?fonum=1130 and http://www.sare.org/Grants.

[248] SARE, "Grant Summaries by State," http://www.sare.org/Grants/Grant-Summaries-by-State. SARE's searchable database is at http://www.sare.org/Project-Reports/Search-the-Database.

Nutrition Assistance Programs

Farmers' Market Nutrition Programs

FNS administers two programs that provide benefits redeemable only at farmers' markets—the WIC Farmers' Market Nutrition Program (WIC-FMNP), and the Senior Farmers' Market Nutrition Program (SFMNP). FNS provides grants to state agencies, such as state health, agriculture, and other agencies and Indian Tribal Organizations (ITOs), in nearly all states.[249] Participating state agencies must submit a plan describing how the agency intends to implement, operate, and administer the program. Grant payments are made by a letter of credit, and state agencies may withdraw funds only as needed.

The WIC-FMNP was first established in 1992 under the Special Supplemental Nutrition Program for Women, Infants and Children (WIC) to provide fresh, locally grown produce to low-income WIC applicants and recipients and to expand their use of farmers' markets. The program allows farmers' markets and roadside stands to accept WIC-FMNP benefits (usually through coupons).[250] Participating state agencies must provide program income or state, local, or private funds for the program in an amount that is equal to at least 30% of the administrative cost of the program, with some exceptions for tribal agencies. In FY2013, the program covered an estimated 1.56 million recipients, and about 17,700 farmers, 3,300 farmers' markets, and 2,800 roadside stands. Coupons redeemed through the program resulted in an estimated $13.2 million in revenue to farmers for FY2013. Total WIC-FMNP grant funding ranged from $19 million to $23 million per year between FY2010 and FY2013; grant amounts for individual states are at USDA's website.[251] Appropriated funding for the WIC FMNP totaled about $16.5 million in FY2014.

The SFMNP was authorized in the 2002 farm bill, and reauthorized in the 2008 farm bill, to provide fruits, vegetables, herbs, and honey from farmers' markets, roadside stands, and CSA programs to low-income seniors, by allowing farmers' markets and roadside stands to accept FMNP coupons.[252] The SFMNP awards grants to states, territories, and ITOs to provide low-income seniors with coupons that can be exchanged for eligible foods at farmers' markets, roadside stands, and CSAs. Funding in FY2013 covered an estimated 836,000 participants and about 20,600 farmers, 4,200 farmers' markets, 3,100 roadside stands, and 190 CSAs. The 2014 farm bill extended the annual mandatory funding, provided by a transfer from the CCC, of $20.6 million annually through FY2018. State-by-state allocations of funds are at USDA's website.[253]

---

[249] A map of participating states is at http://www.fns.usda.gov/wic/SFMNP-FMNP-Map.pdf.

[250] P.L. 111-296, §424; 42 U.S.C. 1786, amending the Child Nutrition Act (CFDA# 10.572). FNS, http://www.fns.usda.gov/wic/fmnp/fmnpfaqs htm.

[251] FNS, "WIC FMNP Profiles – Grants and Participation," http://www fns.usda.gov/wic/wic-fmnp-profiles-grants-and-participation.

[252] P.L. 107-171; §4402; 7 U.S.C. 3007 (CFDA# 10.576). USDA, http://www fns.usda.gov/wic/SeniorFMNP/SFMNPmenu htm.

[253] FNS, "SFMNP Profiles – Grants and Participation," http://www fns.usda.gov/sfmnp/sfmnp-profiles-grants-and-participation.

Supplemental Nutrition Assistance Program (SNAP) at Farmers' Markets

In addition, benefits under the FNS-administered Supplemental Nutrition Assistance Program (SNAP, formerly food stamps) provide additional available resources to patronize and support farmers markets. SNAP participants receive benefits on an electronic benefit transfer card that they may redeem at an authorized retailer for most foods. SNAP benefits may also be used to purchase seeds or plants to grow food.[254] Farmers' markets may become SNAP-licensed retailers.[255] USDA reported that 4,057 farmers' markets or individual farmers were authorized to accept SNAP benefits in FY2013, and they redeemed a total of $21.2 million in SNAP benefits.[256] Compared to FY2012, this is an increase of over 26% in authorizations and almost 28% in benefits redeemed. In FY2013, 49% of the direct-from-farm authorized retailers are in 10 states (California, Iowa, Massachusetts, Michigan, Mississippi, Missouri, New York, Ohio, Oregon, and Pennsylvania). The 2014 farm bill also added language that "allows SNAP to be accepted in advance of food delivery by agricultural producers who market directly to consumers."[257]

SNAP law, however, does not require that benefits be redeemed at local establishments or in farm-to-consumer settings; however, certain policies are related.

The 2014 farm bill provided for SNAP Bonus Incentive Projects and other related grants. States, localities, and farmers' market networks have created SNAP bonus incentive programs to target the redemption of benefits at farmers' markets. These allow SNAP participants to redeem their benefits for more than "money on the dollar." For example, a participant may exchange $3 of benefits for a $6 voucher to redeem at the market. In the past, USDA-FNS, however, required that the bonus funds be non-federal dollars; although, the 2014 farm bill creates a competitive grant program that will provide limited funding for bonus incentives (Food Insecurity Nutrition Incentive grants). Prior to 2010, markets had to apply to FNS for a waiver of the rules through the state SNAP agency. Beginning early in 2010, FNS allowed farmers' markets that secured non-federal bonus incentive funding to be eligible through a blanket waiver, so markets now just report to an FNS field office that they are conducting a bonus incentive program.

Farm to School Program

USDA's Farm to School program was authorized in the Healthy, Hunger-Free Kids Act of 2010, which amended the Richard B. Russell National School Lunch Act (NSLA).[258] The 2010 law included $5 million annually in mandatory funding for the program and also allows for additional discretionary funding. Its goals are geared toward increasing fruit and vegetable consumption

---

[254] The 1973 farm bill (Agriculture and Consumer Protection Act of 1973, P.L. 93-86, 7 U.S.C. §2012(b)) included an amendment to the Food Stamp Act stating that "the term 'food'... shall also include seeds and plants for use in gardens to produce food for the personal consumption of the eligible household." For information see FNS, "SNAP: Eligible Foods," http://www.fns.usda.gov/snap/retailers/eligible.htm and SNAPGardens.org, http://www.snapgardens.org/.

[255] For information see USDA, FNS, "SNAP: Learn How You Can Accept SNAP Benefits at Farmers' Markets," http://www.fns.usda.gov/snap/ebt/fm.htm.

[256] USDA FNS, "SNAP's Benefit Redemption Division (BRD) Annual Report for Fiscal Year 2011," December 2011, http://www.fns.usda.gov/snap/retailers/pdfs/2011-annual-report.pdf.

[257] Quotation from FNS implementation memorandum dated March 21, 2014, http://www.fns.usda.gov/snap/supplemental-nutrition-assistance-program-snap, refers to P.L. 113-79, Section 4012.

[258] P.L. 111-296, §243, 42 U.S.C. §1769 (CFDA# 10.579). See, also, USDA, "Legislative History Related to Farm to School," http://www.fns.usda.gov/cnd/F2S/pdf/F2Sleg_history.pdf.

---

among students, supporting local farmers and rural communities, and providing nutrition and agriculture education to school districts and farmers. The program is administered by FNS.

The Farm to School program provides competitive grants and technical assistance to eligible schools,[259] state and local agencies, ITOs, agricultural producers or groups of agricultural producers, and nonprofit entities to implement farm-to-school programs that improve access to local foods in eligible schools. Grants may be used for training, supporting operations, planning, purchasing equipment, developing school gardens, developing partnerships, and implementing farm-to-school programs. Schools and communities may initiate and support a variety of eligible activities, including nutrition education, agriculture-related lessons and curriculum, school or community gardens, farm tours, taste testing, and parent/community educational sessions.[260] The enacting language further ensured that "geographical diversity" and "equitable treatment of urban, rural, and tribal communities" be considered when USDA awards grants under the program. The statute also includes criteria for selection, including making local food products available on the menu, serving a high proportion of students who receive free and reduced-price meals, incorporating nutrition education, demonstrating collaboration between schools and other community partners, and evaluating the results. Grant amounts are not to exceed $100,000 per recipient, and the federal share is not to exceed 75% of the total project cost.

FNS awarded FY2013 funding[261] and has released a request for applications for FY2014.[262]

USDA's Farm to School summary report highlights the department's findings from its review in 2010 of 15 school districts nationwide that were involved in farm-to-school-related activities.[263] Other information on farm-to-school programs is available through the National Farm to School Network, highlighting activities in each state.[264]

School Gardens

The 2008 farm bill also amended the Richard B. Russell NSLA by authorizing a pilot program of grants for high-poverty schools to promote healthy food education and hands-on gardening in the school curriculum.[265] The pilot program is part of USDA's child nutrition discretionary grants and its goals are geared toward increasing fruit and vegetable consumption among students, supporting local farmers and rural communities, and providing nutrition and agriculture education to school districts and farmers. The program is administered by FNS.

---

[259] An "eligible school" means a school or institution that participates in a program under this act or the school breakfast program established under §4 of the Child Nutrition Act of 1966 (42 U.S.C. 1773).

[260] USDA, FNS, "Farm to School," http://www.fns.usda.gov/cnd/f2s/about.htm#Initiative; also USDA, "USDA Farm to School Initiative Fact Sheet," http://www.fns.usda.gov/cnd/f2s/pdf/F2S_initiative_fact_sheet_040110.pdf.

[261] USDA, FNS, "USDA Farm to School FY 2013 Grant Awards," http://www.fns.usda.gov/cnd/f2s/pdf/F2S_Grants-FY2013.pdf.

[262] USDA, FNS, "Farm to School Grant Program," http://www.fns.usda.gov/cnd/f2s/f2_2013_grant_program.htm.

[263] FNS, *USDA Farm to School Team 2010 Summary Report*, July 2011, http://www.fns.usda.gov/cnd/f2s/pdf/2010_summary-report.pdf.

[264] National Farm to School Network, http://www.farmtoschool.org/aboutus.php.

[265] P.L. 110-246, §4303, 42 U.S.C. §1769 (CFDA# 10.579). The term "eligible school" means a public school where at least 50% of the students are eligible for free or reduced price meals.

The pilot program is to target not more than five states and may be used through either a school-based program or a community-based summer program that is part of, or coordinated with, a summer enrichment program at two or more eligible schools. The farm bill created discretionary funding authority to carry out the program. The pilot program provides for applications to enter into a:

> cooperative agreement for the purposes of developing and running community gardens at eligible high-poverty schools; teaching students involved in the gardens about agriculture production practices, diet, and nutrition; contributing produce to supplement food provided at eligible schools, student households, local food banks, or senior center nutrition programs; and conducting an evaluation of funded projects to learn more about the impacts of school gardens.[266]

USDA has awarded a single grant to Washington State University (WSU), which is expected to serve an estimated 2,800 students attending 70 elementary schools in Washington, New York, Iowa, and Arkansas.[267] WSU extension is the lead institution on the project—called the "Healthy Gardens, Healthy Youth" pilot project—along with the cooperative extension services of Iowa State University, Cornell University, and the University of Arkansas.[268] The project was funded at $1 million in FY2010 under the agency's People's Garden School Pilot Program as part of the USDA People's Garden Initiative to establish community and school gardens nationwide.[269]

Annual appropriations have not provided further funding for these efforts, but FNS has utilized other funding to continue these types of efforts. For example, in FY2011, USDA provided approximately $725,000 in grants for its People's Garden Grant Program, administered by NIFA.[270] This was a new program in 2011, authorized in the National Agricultural Research, Extension, and Teaching Policy Act to facilitate the initial investment needed to create produce, recreation, and/or wildlife gardens in urban and rural areas, and to provide opportunities for science-based non-formal education.[271] In 2011, the program funded 10 projects in Alaska, Arizona, California, Colorado, Connecticut, Hawaii, Maryland, Michigan, and Ohio.[272] Many of these projects include school gardens, among other types of projects.

For FY2015, funding for "Visitor Center/People's Garden" is reported at $0.9 million.[273] In addition, the 2010 reauthorization of the child nutrition programs (P.L. 111-296) further amended this section of the Russell School Lunch Act and extended the authority for appropriations to FY2015. The 2008 farm bill had only authorized activities through FY2012.

---

[266] FNS "People's Garden School Pilot Overview," October 14, 2010, webinar.

[267] USDA, "USDA Announces Funding to Expand School Community Gardens and Garden-Based Learning Opportunities," August 25, 2010; and USDA, "USDA Announces People's Garden School Pilot Program to Promote Garden-Based Learning Opportunities," April 7, 2011.

[268] WSU, "$1 Million Grant Funds WSU Extension 'Healthy Gardens, Healthy Youth' Project," April 7, 2011.

[269] USDA's budget justification for FY2011, http://www.obpa.usda.gov/30fns2011notes.pdf. See page 30-10.

[270] NIFA, "People's Garden Grant Program," http://www.csrees.usda.gov/fo/peoplesgardengrantprogram.cfm. See also USDA, "USDA Expands People's Garden Initiative to Sow Seeds for Community-Based Agriculture across the Country," November 10, 2011.

[271] P.L. 95-113, 7 U.S.C 3318 (b); CFDA# 10.325.

[272] NIFA, "Abstracts of Funded Projects," http://www.csrees.usda.gov/fo/peoplesgardengrantprogram.cfm.

[273] USDA's budget justification for FY2015, http://www.obpa.usda.gov/04da2015notes.pdf. See p. 4-3.

Commodity Procurement Through "DoD Fresh"

The Department of Defense Fresh Fruit and Vegetable Program (DoD Fresh) is a mechanism created by USDA to increase fresh produce offerings to schools. DoD Fresh, which utilizes the logistical capacity of the United States military to deliver food to U.S. military bases across the country and world, began as a USDA pilot project in 1996. States are able to allocate a portion of their commodity entitlement funds for school meals toward procurement of fresh produce through the DOD Fresh program. The DoD Fresh program began as a USDA pilot project in 1996, with eight states participating by allocating a portion of their commodity entitlement funds toward the program. In 1996-1997, DoD Fresh delivered produce valued at about $3.2 million to schools in eight states. By 2010, the DoD Fresh delivered produce valued at $66 million to schools in all 50 states.

The 2008 farm bill amended policies governing USDA's purchase of fresh fruits and vegetables through DoD Fresh.[274] Specifically, the 2008 farm bill amended the National School Lunch Act to "allow institutions ..., including the Department of Defense Fresh Fruit and Vegetable Program, to use a *geographic preference* for the procurement of unprocessed agricultural products, both locally grown and locally raised" (emphasis added) and "encourage institutions ... to purchase unprocessed agricultural products, both locally grown and locally raised, to the maximum extent practicable and appropriate."[275] While the 2008 farm bill provision did not specifically define "locally grown and locally raised," FNS and DOD have generally applied the definition of "locally or regionally produced agricultural food products" established elsewhere in the farm bill,[276] specifically, "any agricultural food product that is raised, produced, and distributed in ... the locality or region in which the final product is marketed, so that the total distance that the product is transported is less than 400 miles from the origin of the product; or ... the state in which the product is produced."[277] As a provision allowing for a preference, DoD Fresh does not require states and school food authorities to purchase local products.

Section 4202 of the 2014 farm bill established a new pilot program for up to eight states to explore procurement alternatives – including local procurement – for unprocessed fruits and vegetables, in place of those commodity purchases offered through DOD.

Healthy Food Financing Initiative

Prior to the 2014 farm bill, the Administration administered a Healthy Food Financing Initiative (HFFI) by requesting appropriations for several existing statutory authorities in order to provide grants and tax credits to support development of food retailers in underserved communities. Since 2010, the Administration has operated related programs at USDA, Health and Human Services (HHS), and/or the U.S. Treasury. See "Healthy Food Financing Initiative"

The 2014 farm bill (P.L. 113-79, § 4206) established a new authority by the same name, Healthy Food Financing Initiative, to "support efforts to provide access to healthy food by establishing an initiative to improve access to healthy foods in underserved areas, to create and preserve quality

---

[274] USDA, http://www.fns.usda.gov/fdd/programs/dod/DOD_FreshFruitandVegetableProgram2011.pdf.

[275] NSLA, §9(j); 42 U.S.C. 1758(j)) amended in 2008 farm bill (P.L. 110-246, §4302). Covers also non-DoD schools.

[276] CRS communication with FNS staff, September 12, 2011.

[277] P.L. 110-246, §6015.

jobs, and to revitalize low-income communities by providing loans and grants to eligible fresh, healthy food retailers to overcome the higher costs and initial barriers to entry in underserved areas."[278] USDA is authorized to approve a community development financial institution as "national fund manager" that would administer these funds by supporting food retail projects that would "expand or preserve access to staple foods" (as defined within this section) and accept SNAP benefits.

The law authorizes up to $125 million to be appropriated for a "Healthy Food Financing Initiative" to remain available until expended.

Community Food Projects

The Community Food Projects (CFP) program (formerly the Community Food Projects Competitive Grants Program) was created in the 1996 and further amended in the 2008 and 2014 farm bills.[279] Administered by NIFA, the program provides grants to support projects that meet the food needs of low-income people, increase the self-reliance of communities in providing for their own needs, and promote comprehensive responses to local food, farm, and nutrition issues. For example, projects linking low-income populations to fresher foods through farmers' markets have previously qualified as activities. The 2008 farm bill reauthorized the competitive grants and funded them at $5 million for FY2008 and each fiscal year thereafter. Activities supported by this program are a wide range of community-based projects and initiatives, including urban agriculture and targeted markets to address food desert communities. Grants are awarded for community food projects, planning projects, and training and technical assistance projects. The range of grant awards and their duration depend on the type of project, but all three types require a match in resources.[280] The 2014 farm bill increased funds for this program by $4 million to a total of $9 million in FY2015 and each fiscal year thereafter. The 2014 law also included new types of eligible grantees, for example "gleaners."

Food Insecurity Nutrition Incentive grants

The 2014 farm bill significantly amended what had been the "hunger-free community grants" to "incentive grants" for projects that incentivize SNAP participants to buy fruits and vegetables, and renamed the incentive grant program the "Food Insecurity Nutrition Incentive."[281] The federal cost share under the program is limited to 50%. The 2014 farm bill provided $100 million in mandatory funding (FY2014-FY2018), plus discretionary authority of $5 million per year.

[278] P.L. 113-79, §4206. Amended Title II, Subtitle D of the Department of Agriculture Reorganization Act of 1994 (7 U.S.C. §§ 6951 *et seq.*).

[279] P.L. 110-246, §4402, 7 U.S.C 2034 (CFDA# 10.225), amending the Food Stamp Act of 1977. See NIFA, http://www.csrees.usda.gov/funding/cfp/cfp_synopsis html and http://www nifa.usda.gov/fo/communityfoodprojects.cfm; and USDA, http://www.usda.gov/wps/portal/usda/usdahome?contentid=kyf_grants_nifa4_content.html.

[280] FY2012 Request for Applications: http://www.csrees.usda.gov/funding/rfas/pdfs/12_community_food.pdf.

[281] P.L. 113-79, § 4208.

Author Contact Information

Renée Johnson
Specialist in Agricultural Policy
rjohnson@crs.loc.gov, 7-9588

Randy Alison Aussenberg
Analyst in Nutrition Assistance Policy
raussenberg@crs.loc.gov, 7-8641

Tadlock Cowan
Analyst in Natural Resources and Rural
Development
tcowan@crs.loc.gov, 7-7600